STUART

WHERE HAVE ALL THE SHEPHERDS GONE?

REDISCOVER THE HEART OF LOVING & LEADING PEOPLE

First published in 2025

Copyright © Stuart Blount 2025
www.stuartblount.com

Published for Stuart Blount by Verité CM Ltd, Worthing, UK

The right of Stuart Blount to be identified as the author of this work has been asserted by him in accordance with the Copyright, Designs and Patents Act 1988.

All rights reserved. No part of this publication may be reproduced, stored in a retrieval system, or transmitted in any other form or by any means, electronic, mechanical, photocopying, recording or otherwise, without the prior permission of the publisher.

ISBN 978-1-914-388-70-5

Unless otherwise marked, Scripture quotations are from the Holy Bible, New International Version (Anglicised edition). Copyright © 1979, 1984, 2011 Biblica. Used by permission of Hodder & Stoughton Ltd, an Hachette UK company. All rights reserved.

Scripture quotations marked 'KJV' are from The Authorised (King James) Version. Rights in the Authorised Version in the United Kingdom are vested in the Crown. Reproduced by permission of the Crown's patentee, Cambridge University Press.

Scripture quotations from *The Message*, copyright © 1993, 2002, 2018 by Eugene H. Peterson. Used by permission of NavPress. All rights reserved. Represented by Tyndale House Publishers, Inc.

Cover Design by Karen Wells
Print Management by Verité CM Ltd
veritecm.com

TESTIMONIALS

With honesty, biblical insight and hard-earned wisdom, Stuart explores what healthy shepherd-leadership might look like in our culture. This book encourages us to renew a desire for humility, integrity and sacrificial service but equally reinforces the need for leaders to be secure, self-aware and properly supported. I would highly recommend this book to younger and more seasoned leaders as well as wider leadership teams. It is a much-needed recalibration as we seek to serve others faithfully and sustainably.

Cathy Madavan
Author, speaker, board member of the Kyria Network and a leader at Fishponds Baptist Church, Bristol

Stuart recently spoke at our church, and his son Matt introduced him with the words, 'It's my honour to introduce my dad and my hero.' Now that's an endorsement! Everywhere I go in the UK I meet pastors who know Stuart, and they all speak highly of his wisdom, humility and heart for people. In recent years, we've heard so much about leadership, discipleship and church growth – but when it comes to shepherding, we seem to have gone silent. This book is a much-needed call back to the heart of pastoring, reminding us that true leadership is not just about strategy and vision, but about loving and leading people well. Stuart has lived this message for decades, and every pastor and leader should read these pages – and embrace the true heart of a shepherd.

Steve Mawston
Leadership Coach, and Elder at Soul Church, Norwich

If there was ever a time for the church to recapture the urgency for the people-centred pastor, the time is now! This book offers authentic insight and story-based examples over many years of ministry. It challenges the church leader to pursue the Chief Shepherd first whilst recognising their responsibility to serve those who they lead.

Dave Newton
National Director, Scripture Union

I love this book, which reminds us of the significance of our call to be shepherds and shepherdesses whose hearts should move ever closer to reflecting God into our homes, churches and world. This should be read by every pastor, from the most experienced to those preparing for ministry. As someone who has seen the parallels between God's people and the character and vulnerability of sheep whilst walking the Welsh hills, I think this book helpfully draws deeply upon Scripture and lived experience, enabling us to reflect not only on our practice but the disposition of our hearts as we pastor.

Michelle Nunn
Principal, Regents Theological College and member of Elim's National Leadership Team

In an era where church leadership often resembles corporate management, Stuart's book arrives as a profound wake-up call. With clarity and conviction, Stuart challenges modern ministry's drift towards event planning and programme management, instead championing a return to the fundamental calling of pastoral care. Drawing on the timeless model of the Good Shepherd, this compelling work reminds us that true leadership flows from a wellspring of love – both for God and for those we serve. Essential reading for anyone in ministry who yearns to move beyond spreadsheets and schedules to rediscover the transformative power of sacrificial, heartfelt shepherding.

Mark Pugh
General Superintendent, Elim Pentecostal Churches

ACKNOWLEDGEMENTS

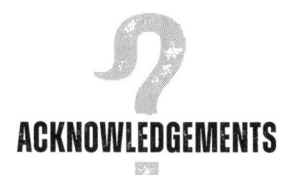

I believe that we can never claim to have achieved anything in life on our own. That is certainly my story. I have benefitted for so many years from people around my life who have often believed in me more than I have believed in myself. It has been their encouragement that has enabled me to work on a project like this book, among other things I have attempted in my life.

Amanda, my faithful and loving wife, has been my biggest cheerleader ever since we first met forty years ago this year. During the thirty-six years of marriage we have shared, she has consistently supported me as we have lived out the call on our life together to love and lead people. She is one of the best examples I know of sacrificial love. She has shown that as a daughter, wife, mum and now as a beautiful nanna to our gorgeous grandchildren. The spouses of shepherd-leaders rarely get the acknowledgement and gratitude they deserve, so, darling, I hope you know that this book could never have been written without you.

Our wonderful children, daughters-in-law and grandchildren are the greatest joy in our life. Thank you for the love and support you show every day and for stirring me to complete this project.

I am grateful to those who have helped take my written thoughts and bring them to life in this book. Louise Stenhouse has helped me greatly with her excellent editorial work and valuable advice on the text. I also appreciate the help of Chris Powell, Rachael Hobbs and Karen Wells at Verité Publishing who have made this process so much easier for me.

I have been blessed with many friends and in particular my Elim friends and family. I have spent every day of my life as part of the Elim family and nearly thirty-eight years as a minister. You will never know how much this movement means to me. We are not perfect, but we are a family, and that has been a source of strength to me through many of the most challenging days of my life. I hope that my colleagues in the Elim ministry will find our shared story in these pages, as we seek to love people and lead them to thrive in this life.

DEDICATION

This book is dedicated to all those I have loved and led. Thank you for your patience and your love in response to my attempts to follow in the footsteps of the Good Shepherd.

CONTENTS

	Foreword	11
	Introduction	15
1.	A Young Man's Journey	23
2.	Who Chooses to be a Shepherd?	33
3.	The Shepherd-Leader	43
4.	An Ancient Job Description	55
5.	The Sheep are in Danger	67
6.	Leading from the Heart	79
7.	The Title or the Towel	91
8.	The Weight of Leadership	103
9.	Wounds and Scars	117
10.	The Shepherd's Superpower	129
11.	The Unwritten Chapter	141
	Endnotes	149

FOREWORD

When I was growing up one of my favourite genres of movies was westerns. It was my mother's fault; she loved westerns and helped me to love them too. It wasn't just the black-and-white classics but in her later life we often went to the cinema together to watch the latest remake of an old classic. I can still hear her saying all through the film, 'It's good but not as good as the John Wayne version!'

There is something enigmatic about cowboys: they're glamorous, adventurous, ruggedly independent often riding off into the sunset alone. If I was asked as a young boy, 'Would you rather be a cowboy or a shepherd?' I wouldn't have to phone a friend! Who wants to be a shepherd if there is a chance you could be a cowboy?

Interestingly, what the Bible uses for its central metaphor for what a leader should look like is a shepherd.

You see, cowboys love being cowboys, but you don't get the sense that they love the cows they're leading. Cowboys drive from behind; they don't lead from in front or alongside like shepherds do. Cowboys focus on control whereas the shepherds focus on care. Cowboys prioritise efficiency while shepherds prioritise relationship. Cowboys stay distant, separate; shepherds remain accessible, close by. In a world obsessed with power, performance and productivity it's easy to drift into a leadership style that's more akin to a cowboy than a shepherd.

Why is this so important in the current cultural moment we find ourselves in?

The current era you and I are living in is an era marked by upheaval, challenge and change. In fact it's been referred to by many as 'permacrisis', a state of almost permanent crisis. When it comes to leadership we are also in a bit of a crisis. In many cases, leaders have forgotten that people are not there for them; they are there for people. Whether someone leads in the local church, business or politics it's possible to love leading more than we love the people we are called to lead. It's possible to love speaking more than having something worthwhile to say. It's possible to love the platform and the position more than the potential of what that platform and position can accomplish in people's lives. It's possible to be more like a cowboy than a shepherd.

Stuart lives for something different.

We have known each other for well over thirty years, both of us leading local churches in the Birmingham area. I have seen first hand in Stuart what a shepherd-leader looks like and have been the recipient of that shepherd-leadership from him in my own life. I have seen in Stuart both a humility and a tenacity, both a gentle spirit and a courageous heart. Shepherds are no pushovers – just try hurting the sheep and you will find out how courageous a shepherd can be!

I love this quote from the end of this book:

> *Your legacy will not be the buildings you have built, the messages you have preached or the books you have written. It will be the people you have loved and the way you have led them.*

This is so true, and, in this book, Stuart takes you on a journey through the Bible, personal story and experience powerfully blending principles, tools and ideas that will help you lead for the benefit of those under your watch and care. As we often say here at Lifecentral Church, 'we want something *for* you not something *from* you'.

The need for true shepherd-leadership has never been greater. People are aching for leaders who truly see, know and love them; the future of Christian leadership depends on reclaiming this biblical model.

For those of you starting out in leadership, let this book inspire, equip and send you on the right road. For those of us who have been on the leadership road for many years, may this book refresh and revitalise us. It's possible to start out in leadership with a posture of serving and end up in the land of entitlement or discouragement. I believe this book will bring you hope as you rediscover the heart of loving and leading people.

Leon Evans
Lead Pastor, Lifecentral Church, Halesowen

INTRODUCTION

The megaphone of social media amplifies their voices. Their faces beam from bestseller lists and conference banners. They lead thousands, command massive followings, and shape Christian culture with each tweet or post. Yet in the shadow of these celebrity pastors, a question echoes through empty church offices and quiet buildings: Where have all the shepherds gone?

I've watched this transformation over decades of ministry. What was once a calling centred on knowing your flock by name has, in many places, morphed into a model that prizes platform over presence, influence over intimacy. While I appreciate many aspects of modern church leadership and the opportunities that technology brings, I can't shake the conviction that something essential is being lost – the heart of the shepherd.

This isn't about nostalgia for a bygone era. It's about a fundamental tension at the core of Christian leadership today: the gap between the spectacle of success and the quiet work of shepherding souls. As someone who has navigated both worlds, I've seen first hand how this shift affects not just leaders, but the very people they're called to serve.

The genesis of this book goes back many years to 2011, when the General Superintendent of the Elim Churches in the UK, John Glass, invited me to talk about shepherd-leadership at the annual conference for Elim's Ministers in Training. I like to think that John asked me to speak on this topic because of what he had seen demonstrated in my own life and ministry. If so, then this is one of the biggest compliments ever afforded to me. What it did do, was to focus me on seeking to understand what was one of the challenges the church was facing, that is, a lack of emphasis on the shepherding responsibilities of local church pastors. I think it is still one of our challenges today.

It's still the case that most people who are blessed to follow a calling to lead a local church community will never lead more than a hundred people. Even in the USA, where some believe every other corner has a mega church, the median size of weekly Sunday church gatherings is only sixty-five.[1] What is the significance of this? Well, it's simply to remind us that our calling is not to fulfil a quota. It's to love and lead people well. That is what this book is about. Whether you carry responsibility for ten people or ten thousand people the critical question is about whether we are loving and leading them well.

A SHEPHERDING CRISIS IN THE MODERN CHURCH

I am often sickened by the excesses of a small number of Christian leaders who have made themselves super rich and do so whilst justifying their greed from the scriptures. I know these people are in a minority, but I'm going to say it – it's wrong. Well, I may have just lost some readers before we've even exited the introduction. However, I am not aiming to write something that earns me friends or favours, but rather that addresses at least some of the issues that plague the Western, mostly evangelical/charismatic church.

Sheep need shepherds. People need leaders, and the two are not mutually exclusive. This is the primary thesis of this book. To shepherd is to lead and to lead is to shepherd. Both are all about people. Lost people and saved people – just people. Precious people; hurting people; sinful people. Quite simply, people who Jesus loves. Yet I have seen an exclusivity develop in many leadership settings that has set some leaders apart from those they are supposed to be leading.

I think they've forgotten that leadership in the church is the leadership of people. Sadly, some might not have started out with the compelling call to love and lead people; they might have begun their journey into leadership with aspirations of popularity and significance. I'm convinced that to love people and to lead them are the same thing, not two opposing styles of leadership.

This is my heart's message as I write. I have reviewed my own years serving Jesus as a leader, and I can see the mistakes I made when pursuing success and recognition, sometimes at the expense of the people who sat in front of me every weekend. I can see moments when I was impatient for them to change or to adopt my latest idea or jump into the latest venture with abandoned enthusiasm. Don't get me wrong, I loved those I served. I've always loved people and being with people (well, there may have been a few exceptions along the way – hey, I'm only human).

I know that as a young leader I was desperate to see the churches I led grow, and growth was almost exclusively understood as an increase in the number of people attending church services on a Sunday. That's not wrong because a fuller definition of success in ministry acknowledges that the advance of the kingdom of God is about seeking lost people and leading them to Jesus. But advancing the kingdom is also about discipling them to be like Jesus and then equipping them to join the shared mission of finding more lost people, and so the cycle continues.

If people ever lose their value to us, the value that they hold with Jesus, then we're in trouble. It's knowing that they are his, not ours, and that we carry a spiritual responsibility for their wellbeing, that helps shape the kind of healthy values that will keep good shepherd-leaders from problematic pathways, some of which we'll look at later.

SHAPED BY PERSONAL EXPERIENCE

I think that my generation of leaders here in the UK have bridged two quite different worlds when it comes to local church leadership. I have painted some brief biographical experiences in the next chapter that illustrate my own early experiences of pastors. It was for me a positive experience, and I realise how blessed I was.

The models I saw in the two pastors I had growing up were different, even though they were not too far apart in age from one another. One was in every way a wonderful pastor who gently led an ageing and traditional congregation into a new and modern building. He wisely sought to deepen the faith and hunger for God of that church family, who, to be honest, often demonstrated parochial attitudes and behaviour as family allegiances made change a huge challenge. My second pastor deeply impacted me. He was young, in his early thirties, and had been personally impacted by the charismatic renewal of the late 1970s and early 1980s in the UK. He led with enthusiasm and passion for God which, as a fifteen-year-old, ignited my own passion for God.

I am not suggesting that all church leaders have abandoned their pastoral posts or priorities. In posing the question 'Where have all the shepherds gone?' I am not presuming that those in Christian leadership have all forsaken the people they lead. I am, however, acknowledging that for a generation now (certainly in the Western church) there has been an emphasis on becoming a great leader, sometimes with no definition of what that is supposed to look like. I am particularly highlighting the preoccupation with the image of leadership over the heart of a shepherd.

I am thankful that the denomination I have served for nearly four decades isn't overly concerned with titles, because I do know of some other streams of the church where this seems hugely important. Apostle, prophet, evangelist, teacher and even pastor are not titles in scripture. They are 'graces' or 'gifts' given to the body of Christ 'to equip his people for works of service, so that the body of Christ may be built up' (Ephesians 4:12). But of course, you know that. But why are so many still preoccupied with being called the right thing or the next thing? Jesus spoke of the Pharisees' obsession with titles, position and honour:

> *The teachers of the law and the Pharisees sit in Moses' seat. So, you must be careful to do everything they tell you. But do not do what they do, for they do not practise what they preach. They tie up heavy, cumbersome loads and put them on other people's shoulders, but they themselves are not willing to lift a finger to move them. Everything they do is done for people to see: they make their phylacteries wide and the tassels on their garments long; they love the place of honour at banquets and the most important seats in the synagogues; they love to be greeted with respect in the market-places and to be called 'Rabbi' by others. But you are not to be called 'Rabbi', for you have one Teacher, and you are all brothers.* (Matthew 23:2-8)

A CALL TO RETURN TO AUTHENTIC SHEPHERD-LEADERSHIP

I've been to a few places. And by that, I mean I've seen some of the well-known modern personalities of the Western church. I've visited some of their churches and conferences and seen how the trappings of celebrity are played out in those environments. Ironically, I have seen similar things in much smaller settings.

I know that there are many thousands, even tens of thousands, of women and men who serve in Christian ministry who are living vicariously for the wellbeing of those they lead. It's just that we rarely hear about them. Their stories aren't as glamorous as the mega church pastors or those whose personal YouTube profile holds great importance for them.

The pattern given to us by the Shepherd God alone determines what loving well and leading well looks like. He has given us sufficient evidence in the description of himself and his example as the Good Shepherd throughout scripture that we can model ourselves on, and we will explore some of this evidence in these pages.

The heart of shepherd-leadership isn't measured in followers, figures or Facebook likes. It's found in the faithful presence of those who know that every face in their congregation represents a soul Christ died to save. Whether you shepherd ten people or ten thousand, the calling remains the same: to love deeply, lead wisely and walk alongside those in your care.

As we venture deeper into the twenty-first century, the church doesn't need more celebrities – it needs shepherds who will brave the mess and mystery of people's lives. Leaders who understand that success isn't built on the platform of personality, but in the trenches of genuine pastoral care. Those who recognise that their authority comes not from titles or YouTube viewers, but from their willingness to model the servant leadership of Jesus himself.

The chapters that follow will explore a model of shepherd-leadership that I believe is rooted in the character of God and the teaching of the early apostles as they established the leadership values for the church. I also aim to highlight some of the challenges that today's shepherd-leaders face. Their life is not always an easy one, whilst at the same time there is enormous blessing in serving God and the advance of his church. I hope and pray that these pages will inspire an honest self-reflection among those who are either already shepherds in the church, or those who aspire to follow this call.

I have included some short stories within some of the chapters. They are not fictional, they are some of the moments that have impacted my own developing journey as a shepherd-leader. The idea was inspired by my memories of reading a book by one of the Elim leaders I looked up to most throughout my ministry. John Lancaster wrote *Pastor's Casebook* in 1979 to catalogue his experiences as a pastor. That book inspired me to believe that I could love and lead people, even when it wasn't going to be easy.

My memoirs are similarly personal to my pastoral experience, and in a few I have changed names to appropriately protect those whose stories are personal to them.

This book is an urgent call to rediscover the heart of shepherd-leadership. In the pages that follow, we'll explore what it means to truly lead as Jesus led – not from a distance, but up close, where you can smell the sheep. The question isn't just: Where have all the shepherds gone? The real question is: Will you be one who answers the call to return? Will you join the quiet revolution of leaders who measure success not by the size of their platform, but by the depth of their care? The church is waiting. The sheep are listening. And the Good Shepherd is still calling those who will tend his flock with the same love that led him to lay down his life for them.

The path of shepherd-leadership may not lead to acclaim or accolades. But it leads to something far more precious – the deep satisfaction of knowing you've truly cared for Christ's people as he intended. That journey begins now.

1
A YOUNG MAN'S JOURNEY

I never expected to spend thirty years as a local church pastor. In fact, during my teenage years I had little aspiration for anything at all. I grew up in church, part of a large extended Christian family, which meant that my childhood and teenage years were dominated by our family's commitment to the traditional Pentecostal church that was the centre of our social life, as much as our spiritual life.

A VIEW FROM THE BACK ROW

As I grew up, I became more aware that the pastor of the church was appreciated in proportion to how happy the church members were with him, the various services he led and his commitment to visit them in their homes. Church life had a routine in those days, which meant that when the church secretary got up every Sunday evening to make the announcements for the week, they were pretty much always the same. This moment was always meaningful for me because until my mid-teens my grandfather was church secretary, and I would always notice how uncomfortable he seemed to feel doing this week by week. Our pastors had to navigate the precarious politics of deacons' meetings, Annual General Meetings and even family rivalries, which were probably the real pressure points for him.

It may seem a bleak picture of what church was, but the truth is for many a pastor it was quite bleak at times. My earliest memories of a pastor are very positive. I knew nothing else but church life, and I mean nothing else, because my opportunities to play sport outside of school were zero and going to the cinema would apparently have brought the wrath of God on my young head. The two pastors I remember most from my childhood and youth made a deep impression on me personally, and on my notion of what it meant to lovingly lead people.

SHAPED BY THE SHEPHERD'S INFLUENCE

The first pastor I can remember was Bob McDonald, and his lovely wife Edith. Apart from her gorgeous cakes, which were the crowning glory of every church function, I remember Bob's kindness and concern for those he led. It was he who baptised me as a twelve-year-old and modelled leadership with a gentle spirit and deep concern for the church family. I don't remember about how good a preacher he might or might not have been, but I do remember that everyone loved him, or so it seemed to me. In many ways, he was the archetypal shepherd of his generation. Caring, considerate, warm and deeply committed to the well-being of those he led.

As I reflect many years on, I can see that at the core of my philosophy of ministry is this image of a shepherd who cares, but, more to the point, that care is obvious to those they lead. I also consider how the shepherd-leader must develop skills in diplomacy, something I certainly believe Bob seemed to have in great measure. The local church community is like no other environment I have experienced. There are not the dynamics that most people experience in their jobs, where the authority structures are evident and even tied to the contractual obligations an employee must have to those who pay their wages.

The local church is a community of people with a lot of shared values. There is so much that everybody agrees they believe together. In fact, those who would not share those beliefs might eventually feel uncomfortable in a particular church. But the same community can be plagued with a lot of different perspectives on how their church life should happen. From different approaches to worship, to who should be a leader. These were certainly some of the tensions I observed in my childhood, that my pastors were challenged by.

When I was fifteen there was a change of pastor, the first time I can remember this momentous transition in the life of a church. The truth is as young people we were all very excited. Our new pastor was young, energetic and funny. Barry Killick at that stage was known to us for the youth rallies he often spoke at and the way that his energy lifted the environment of the worship, which to be fair was in desperate need of some new life. Barry married Susan not long after coming to our church, and I remember them inviting the youth group around to the church manse and allowing us to write on the walls before they wallpapered them.

These early experiences in church life didn't just shape my understanding of pastoral ministry – they laid the foundation for what I would later discover about authentic shepherd-leadership. While I watched pastors navigate church politics and family dynamics as a youth, I couldn't have known that God was already preparing me for my own journey in ministry. The most profound lesson would come through my own experience as a struggling teen.

Barry's impact on me was far more personal. I had struggled throughout my teens to follow Jesus whilst wanting to be accepted by my school mates as being just like them, which I wasn't. I ended up in a difficult situation that became the main topic of gossip in the church and knocked my self-esteem to an all-time low. My behaviour with a young lady in the church became the main topic of gossip for a few months, but the impact on me lasted much longer. I was a sheep on the fringes of the flock and in real danger of wandering away from church, and probably God, until a shepherd showed genuine interest in me. Not just in my personal wellbeing but in my spiritual potential.

Barry gave me some healthy boundaries and wise words, but he did more than that: he took a chance on me. He got me leading worship and a small group when I was only seventeen, and because of his advice I went to Bible college a few months short of my nineteenth birthday. I will always remember that season in my life. Not for my own young failures, but because somebody cared for me enough to be honest with me, to give me guidance and show that he believed in me. He was my pastor, my shepherd-leader.

I would remember how Barry led me through that season many times over the years, and particularly when I was sitting opposite someone who had made a mess of their life, or at risk of going off the rails. One young man I watched grow up during my CLC days was an example of this. He, like me, grew up in a Christian home, but in his later teen years drifted from his spiritual moorings in quite a significant way. We did, however, see a wonderful turn around for him and were able a little later to support him to go to Bible college. Sadly, this didn't go as well as he had hoped and there came a point when he had to leave the college and come home to Birmingham. I vividly remember his mum coming to me to ask if I could help him as he was struggling with the mistakes he'd made, and knowing that I was only able to help him because of how Barry had supported me. Today that young man is thriving in ministry, and, with his wife, leading a great church, bringing hope and healing to others himself as that commitment to simply *be there* when people need us most is passed on.

Neither of my pastors were perfect. Like every shepherd they were seeking to serve God and his people. They couldn't have known at the time the way their example and concern had a profound effect upon a young man with no sense of direction in his life and who felt on the fringes of every environment he was in. That is the power of shepherding, often unseen but nevertheless deeply significant. Every time we show an interest in someone who we are privileged to lead, we leave a fingerprint on their life that they may never forget.

I suppose that's why I really wanted to write this book. After decades now of loving and leading people, I've realised that despite the many mistakes I have made I have been privileged to play a part in people's exploration of God and their walk with him. On many occasions I had no awareness of the impact that my leadership may well have had, but that's not the point; it's that somehow God in his grace has allowed me, just like he will you, to learn how to lead his people into places where they can flourish and thrive.

My early enthusiasm for preaching, while valuable, was only the beginning of understanding true shepherd-leadership. It was in Swansea, under Denis Phillips' mentorship, that I would begin to grasp the fuller dimensions of what it meant to truly care for God's people. The transition from Bible college theory to pastoral reality would teach me lessons no classroom could.

THE APPRENTICE YEARS

When I first set out on the pathway that would propel me into church leadership, I wasn't motivated by impacting people's lives as much as by the excitement of being able to preach. I confess that in my latter years in Bible college in my preparations to enter pastoral ministry, few things motivated me as much as the opportunity to share God's word. Of course, that's not wrong, but at twenty-one years of age there was much for me to learn about what God was looking for in me as a leader to whom he would entrust the wellbeing of people.

I had that first opportunity to begin to learn what it was like to be a shepherd-leader when I moved to Swansea in South Wales in the late summer of 1987. I'd been visiting the church as a student during my third year of studies and began to build a relationship with the pastor of the church, Denis Phillips. It really did help that Swansea was only twelve miles from Llanelli, where my girlfriend lived. Amanda and I had met at the annual Elim Conference two years before. It really was the provision of God that my first posting to a church was so close to where she lived so that we could develop our relationship and begin our lifelong journey together serving God.

Starting out as an assistant pastor alongside Denis gave me the best opportunity I could have ever asked for to truly understand what the heart of a shepherd-leader looked like. Denis was, and is, deeply committed to a daily walk with the Holy Spirit, and that alone profoundly affected not only how I would lead but how I have lived. Denis and Ronaldine welcomed Amanda and me into their family, and we saw behind their front door just how much they loved and cared for the people God had called them to lead. I suppose it was our first introduction to that part of the shepherd's life few people ever see: their home life.

I think sometimes church people forget that a shepherd is also a spouse and a parent who relies on the privacy and security of family life to recover from the demands and pressures of always caring for others. Those early days hold great fondness for me, and in so many ways I have wished I could go back and extract more from them as I shadowed Denis everywhere, whether on the church platform or visiting people in their homes, hospitals and prisons.

While Denis had shown me the heart of a shepherd-leader, God was about to teach me how to develop my own. At twenty-four years old, stepping into leadership at High Wycombe would challenge everything I thought I knew about pastoral ministry. This season would reveal that shepherd-leadership isn't just about what we do for people, but about who we become in the process.

FINDING MY OWN FEET AS A SHEPHERD

We eventually moved from Swansea to lead a small Elim church in High Wycombe in early 1990, not far from London. It was a daunting adventure to be picking up this responsibility at only twenty-four years of age. Amanda and I were settling into married life having only begun our marital journey seven months before our induction at the church. When I reflect on the four years that we served in High Wycombe, I can see with the advantage of hindsight that it was an assignment designed to teach me so much more about the value of people.

We didn't see the explosive expansion of the church that I longed for and prayed for, but I know my own heart and capacity were stretched by the week-to-week lessons I learned as such a young man in caring for and supporting a wonderful group of people, most of whom were older than I was. Those years, though difficult in many financial and practical ways, taught me that shepherd-leadership is so much more than sermon preparation. It taught me that people are all very different and carry unique, original stories. It taught me that people love and serve God in all kinds of different ways and that the church can make a difference in its community in simple ways.

Those four years in High Wycombe, though not marked by the dramatic growth I had dreamed of, proved to be essential preparation for what lay ahead. When we moved to Birmingham, I brought with me not just experience, but a deeper understanding that true shepherd-leadership is built on valuing people above programmes. The next twenty-three years would build on this foundation in ways I could never have imagined. I confess I didn't appreciate at the time all that God was teaching me until in 1994 we moved to Birmingham to take up the leadership of Christian Life Centre. The years I was privileged to pastor CLC, as we were more commonly known, shaped my life as much as my ministry in so many significant ways, and many of the stories I share within this book come from those two decades of leadership in Birmingham.

FULL CIRCLE: SHEPHERDING SHEPHERDS

Like all seasoned leaders I have learned through my mistakes as much as I have through any successes, but that's pretty much what life is like. In the pages that follow I want to unpack as much of that learning as I can. I will intersperse it with more of the stories of my own experiences along the way, and I hope to inspire younger generations of leaders to see that keeping people at the centre of what we do for God is the most rewarding way to lead.

The church faces huge challenges in this generation, and it would be easy to become consumed with them to the point that we may want to just give up. That is why I have chosen to write this book now. I'm at a time in my life where I long to influence a generation of men and women to pursue this life of shepherd-leadership and have reflected on the reasons why a book like this is important.

I recognise there has for some time now been a changing emphasis on the role of the pastor in the Western church. Everybody wants to be a leader and a preacher, but fewer people want to be a shepherd. I have also seen the effects of bad shepherds and absent shepherds. Too often leaders have seen people as the means to achieve their own ambitions and not the very reason for leadership in the first place. But I suppose, in the main, my motivation is generated from the depth of satisfaction I still feel from loving and leading people to fulfil the potential God has sewn into their life.

Fewer things have brought me greater joy in my many years of ministry than to see the men and women whose lives I have shared in, continue to grow in God and serve him in a wide range of settings, not just in church leadership. Sometimes doing good to people is of itself utterly rewarding. I love how the apostle Paul encourages the believers across Galatia: 'Therefore, as we have opportunity, let us do good to all people, especially to those who belong to the family of believers' (Galatians 6:10).

My journey from the back pew of a traditional Pentecostal church to shepherding congregations of my own has taught me something profound: true shepherd-leadership isn't just a role we step into – it's a transformation of the heart that reshapes everything we do. Through the patient mentoring of leaders like Bob McDonald, Barry Killick and Denis Phillips, I learned that doing good to people isn't just a biblical principle – it's the very heartbeat of pastoral ministry. But this is only the beginning of the story.

In the chapters ahead, we'll explore how the timeless principles of shepherd-leadership speak to our contemporary challenges. We'll examine what it means to lead with both strength and tenderness, to balance vision with vulnerability, and to guide God's people in an age that often values metrics over ministry. Whether you're a seasoned pastor or just beginning to sense God's call to shepherd his flock, the journey ahead will challenge our assumptions about leadership while deepening our understanding of what it truly means to walk in the footsteps of the Good Shepherd.

WHO CHOOSES TO BE A SHEPHERD?

I can still remember sitting in an old hall in Digbeth in Birmingham city centre. I was there with other young people from my church for a special weekend led by Operation Mobilisation. I'm not sure why I agreed to go because I didn't have a passion for world mission, but I think when you're seventeen years old and get the chance to go away with other young people for a weekend, you grasp it. That weekend changed the course of my life. In fact, the whole six months leading up to that weekend changed the course of my life.

In the summer I had gone away with others from my church to the Dales Bible Week at the Harrogate Showground in beautiful North Yorkshire. At that time the church in the UK was being shaken by what was known as the charismatic movement. For nearly twenty years God had been moving in the historic denominations in the UK whilst the traditional Pentecostal movements thought that they had a monopoly on the moving of the Holy Spirit. Of course, that notion of exclusivity on the Holy Spirit was crazy. The way in which a whole new move of God was bringing amazing freedom in worship, a renewal of church communities and a rediscovery of the gifts and ministry of the Spirit was changing the landscape of the church in the UK.

I vividly remember one evening meeting in a packed cowshed used for rural shows ordinarily but, in this instance, it was a meeting place for thousands of thirsty worshippers. I was captivated by the presence of God in a way I had never known before. As thousands of people sang a refrain simply declaring 'Hosanna', I felt like heaven was being unfolded around me. I wept profusely as, for the first time in my life, I got a glimpse of the enormity and magnificence of God for myself. I realised that my life could be so much more, and something was lit inside me that has never gone out.

By the time I arrived in Digbeth Town Hall that same autumn, I was desperately trying to understand what God wanted me to do with my life. I hadn't talked to anybody about this compelling feeling I had that God wanted to do something with my life, I just kept asking God to show me, maybe expecting some audible voice – which, to be honest, would have frightened the life out of me – or maybe even a letter from God, addressed specifically to me. I don't remember much at all about the weekend, apart from sleeping on a cold church-hall floor in Alum Rock, and the certainty inside me that I was called to serve the Lord Jesus.

I am writing this just a few days after hearing that George Verwer, the founder of OM, has gone to be with the Lord. He was an inspirational character and that weekend he caught my imagination with his jacket emblazoned with the map of the world and his call to us young people to serve Jesus in the advance of world mission. I came away from that weekend knowing I was called by God. It would be a year later that I would understand more clearly that I was called to pastoral ministry during my first year at Elim Bible College. But the certainty awakened in me in the autumn of 1983 in central Birmingham has never left me.

There isn't any doubt that those two occasions were the most significant encounters with God I had experienced. Meeting God in such a personal way is often the birthplace of amazing things in our lives. My small epiphany, though, is dwarfed by the remarkable moment that a young shepherd boy discovers that his future has already been decided by Yahweh, the God of Israel.

Our first encounter with David in the Bible gives us one of these great stories. The youngest of Jesse's eight sons is not at home when the prophet

Samuel does a house visit. David is caring for his father's sheep. I love the analogy contained here. David's preoccupation is with the wellbeing of those his father cared for. Yet it was the qualities that made David good at this specific role in the family that set him apart from his older, bigger and stronger brothers. I wonder if we have got it all mixed up. Have we thought that the leaders God calls are the strongest ones? Or are they the ones who don't get into the line-up when the prophet turns up unannounced?

I'm sure we've all heard a sermon on God's explanation to Samuel for choosing David:

> *Do not consider his appearance or his height, for I have rejected him. The LORD does not look at the things people look at. People look at the outward appearance, but the LORD looks at the heart.* (1 Samuel 16:7)

The calling of God is still a mystery in so many ways and the greatest mystery to me is that he continues to trust us to care for one another. After all, we are just sheep, you know. I've met too many leaders who get ahead of themselves and forget that we all need shepherding. I know more clearly than I ever have how much I need to be shepherded too, and I am so grateful for the leaders in my life who care for me as an extension of the ministry of the Good Shepherd.

The call of God is something that has often been presented in a mysterious fashion. Some have been frightened away from what God has created them to do for him by the idea that only a euphoric moment or divine encounter is sufficient to convince them. I love how Brad Lomenick describes the symbiotic relationship between our true sense of identity and calling:

> *Many people conflate calling with identity. They confuse who they are with what they are made to do. While the two are connected, they are not the same. Identity is who you are, but calling is your purpose . . . It is, according to one of the most*

> *widely accepted definitions, where your deepest passions and your greatest strengths intersect.[2]*

I've reviewed my life through a very different lens as I've got older. I can see that I was called before I was born. Like Jeremiah (Jeremiah 1:5) there was a divine purpose ordained for me long before December 1965 when I was born. This is the essence of calling; a divine purpose that eventually dawns on you and determines everything else you will experience in life.

CALLING: CHOICE OR CHOSEN?

I did not choose to be a shepherd-leader, I was chosen. After decades of loving and leading God's people I understand more clearly that the capacity for such a challenge was already within me, I just had not seen it myself, and, to be honest, I do not think many other people did. That is what is so amazing about the call of God. He takes the often unseen and overlooked, even the most unlikely of characters, and makes something great come out of their lives. He has invested all that he has in bringing his lost children home and continues to look for men and women who will work with him in shepherding their journey whilst here in this life on planet earth.

Jack Hayford, a shepherd-leader I greatly respected, said: 'The role of shepherds is too rarely valued.'[3] I really do agree with him. Especially as I have observed during my journey of ministry the focus shift so dramatically to other styles of leadership in the church. The church goes in cycles, certainly in my experience. Pastors were at one time considered an honoured calling, the pinnacle of one's spiritual journey. Then came a focus on the leader, the 'I'm not pastoral' leader, where dynamic and charismatic leadership skills with entrepreneurial abilities set a person apart as a great leader.

There's nothing wrong with being a great leader if people truly want to follow you. The problem is that some leaders have no rear-view mirrors. They don't ever take a glance to see who is following them as they plough on with directional instructions about where they are headed. But things are changing. Too often entrepreneurial and visionary leaders are facing accusations of narcissism. Apparent great contemporary leaders are discovered to be people who are careless, both as a term for the lack of caution in how they live but also describing the shortfall in the value they have for people.

Tom Nelson challenges some of the notions that have appeared over the last few decades about celebrity leaders in the church: 'Jesus does not offer shepherds a green room to pridefully bask in; instead, he offers a cross and a basin and towel to serve with.'[4] In today's leadership world there are some who ache for the kind of celebrity status that a few leaders possess. It's disheartening to see the lengths that some leaders go to in promoting themselves, especially now that social media offers a free platform to speak from.

There are many privileges that come from leadership in the church, but authentic shepherd-leadership is concerned with fulfilling the responsibilities that have been given by God for the care and wellbeing of his people. This includes their flourishing, growing and reproduction, extending the size of the flock. But all that starts with the right level of nourishment, concern and protection that every follower of Christ needs from those that lead them. Shepherd-leaders see the possibilities in people, but they also do see the needs that people have.

I have observed too many pastors trying to model their style of leadership after mega church leaders who now appear not just on specific Christian TV channels but across YouTube and social media, painting a picture of inspired, charismatic, powerful leadership. What most of us never see are the wreckages of people's lives that lie in the wake of those efforts to maintain such influence and image.

The shepherd call is not to organisational leadership. To lead well involves good organisational skills but the shepherd call is always to lead people. It is people centred, people focused, and people driven. To suggest that Jesus' ministry was not people centred is frankly ridiculous. He walked the length and breadth of what we call the Holy Land to be in people's communities and homes. He entered the celebrations of their lives and their tragedies.

When Jairus urged him to come to his home and lay hands on his daughter, Jesus turned immediately to follow the man but equally had time for a desperately needy woman who grabbed hold of the bottom of his coat, aching to find relief from her years of suffering. Even when an officer in the Roman occupying army asked Jesus to speak a word of healing over his servant, Jesus did not distinguish between this man who represented an enemy of Israel and the need that the man had. Just a cursory reading of the gospels demonstrates that the greatest leader the world has ever seen gave himself fully to the people he came to serve.

I am more convinced that this kind of leadership is what thrives and survives. I believe that strategy and vision are important components in the direction and guidance of a community, but they will fade very quickly without that being smothered by intentional interest in those we ask us to help fulfil such vision.

IT'S A TOUGH JOB BUT SOMEONE'S GOT TO DO IT

In our contemporary age we value the work of shepherds. We understand their skills in rearing sheep. However, ancient shepherds were considered to occupy the bottom rung of society. In fact, very often they didn't own the sheep they cared for. Often, they looked after sheep out in the wild countryside on behalf of owners who probably lived nearby. We see this exampled in David but also in Moses and Jacob who both cared for the sheep owned by their fathers-in-law. These leaders did their apprenticeship for leadership in the shepherding business. The idea that most shepherds did not own the sheep is something Paul reminds the leaders of the church in Ephesus about: 'Keep watch over yourselves and all the flock of which the Holy Spirit has made you overseers. Be shepherds of the church of God, which he bought with his own blood' (Acts 20:28).

I think we have sometimes forgotten this in all the excitement and endeavour of trying to build great churches. I remember hearing one popular leader of a growing church in the UK say, 'People get on the bus and people get off the bus.' I sensed he neither knew nor cared about who was on his bus if they didn't complain about where he was driving the bus. At the time, the church he led was the latest exciting thing going on and people were heading to his leadership conference and seeking to model what they were seeing and hearing. Yet at the same time, behind the scenes were concerns about nepotism and people being driven to volunteer more and more, so that this great thing that was happening could keep growing. Sadly, I know of casualties from that season in that church. People are not a commodity to make a leader look better. They are the children of God 'which he bought with his own blood' (Acts 20:28).

When you read of shepherds in the Bible you see that it was a tough job. There was isolation as they led sheep between various feeding pastures and water sources. And all of this happened in different weather conditions, from the heat of the summer to freezing nights spent on mountain tops protecting the sheep from prowling predators. Some scholars now challenge the notion that shepherds in the time of Christ were a despised group of social outcasts. What cannot be challenged, however, is that their life wasn't easy, nor was it particularly profitable.

Of course, this isn't the life today of a spiritual shepherd, but it does have some parallels. One can feel isolated and vulnerable, I certainly did on many occasions. Though surrounded by family and friends I experienced the deep feeling of responsibility for the wellbeing of the church. I was aware that so much rested on my shoulders, on decisions I needed to make and, most of all, the pressure of keeping my own spiritual life afloat so I could care for and feed others. I also knew what spiritual attack felt like. That invisible threat of personal criticism or division among those I led rarely went away all the years I led a local church family. Over time I learned how to not carry that on my own. I knew who I could talk to for advice and which friends I could count on to support me. Nevertheless, there is always the inner call to be a man or woman who can see the needs of those you are leading above your own.

There is something unique among professions and vocations in the calling to be a shepherd-leader. Many people have jobs and careers that ask many hours' work of them, with bosses who demand high levels of performance, but the call to shepherd the church of Jesus engages us in a spiritual battle that has raged since before time began. This doesn't make shepherd-leaders better people; it simply means we need to be men and women who understand the high calling on our lives.

PEOPLE, PEOPLE, PEOPLE

As I have already said, it is ludicrous to suggest that Jesus' model of leadership was anything other than completely people centred. It is not always reasonable to compare New Testament practice with our modern era because life is vastly different. However, the whole essence of the gospel and the mission of Jesus was, and is, the transformation of humanity person by person. When given the opportunity to read the scriptures in his home synagogue, Jesus chooses to outline his mandate, his mission, his ministry, in the words first given to the prophet Isaiah:

> *The Spirit of the Lord is on me, because he has anointed me to proclaim good news to the poor. He has sent me to proclaim freedom for the prisoners and recovery of sight for the blind, to set the oppressed free, to proclaim the year of the Lord's favour.* (Luke 4:18-19)

Can there be any doubt that those who want to be like Jesus should see the emphasis he gave to meeting the needs of people in body, soul and spirit?

Tom Nelson writes, 'The shepherd leader is a highly relational calling. If people are not your thing, then pastoring should not be your thing.'[5] If you are at the early stages of your life as a shepherd-leader it would serve you well to pause and reflect on this point alone. Your sermons are important, as is creating meaningful times of worship and prayer, but please never forget the people who engage in all these collective activities. Walk among them, talk to them, learn about them, and remember that it is this kind of relationship building that the leader engages in that makes the greatest impression and can have the greatest impact. As I look back over four decades of pastoral ministry, I can see so many faces that I was privileged to get to know. These people are the fruit of my ministry, as they will be of yours.

I recently got a message from a young lady who I pastored in my last church. I haven't seen her since the day of my farewell, but she was one of the last people I baptised a few months before I left to take up my current role. She got in touch to ask if I would conduct her wedding. She doesn't go to the church anymore, so when she wanted to plan her wedding, she could have easily found another minister to conduct her special ceremony, but asked me. It's heart-warming when you realise that the simplest of interests we show in people's lives and their journey with God can have long-lasting impact.

Finding that certainty of calling is critical to the fruitfulness of life as a shepherd-leader. Knowing that the Good Shepherd calls us is the foundation upon which we build our ministry. It's what Jack Hayford expresses as the 'call from beyond':

> *No humanly conspired or psychologically generated source or power can explain this phenomenon. It is more than a mysterious human motivation; it is a mighty and heavenly*

> *one – 'a call from beyond by the One above all!' Nothing else could cause capable, intelligent men and women to leave or refrain from more profitable or more socially accepted enterprises.[6]*

Maybe now is a moment to pause in the presence of God and measure that calling. You may be exploring the call of God on your life and need to hear the divine voice in your soul confirming that he has chosen you for this great task. You may already have known that clarity from God but need reminding today how high and holy that calling is. Or, like me, you may have many years of experience but want to thank God afresh that it is his calling to love and lead people that has carried you this far and will lead you forward.

Whatever place you are at, know with a certainty that this ministry we carry is from him and for him above all else. Let that guide you and shape your ministry so that he is pleased with how you fulfil the purpose he has sewn into our hearts.

THE SHEPHERD-LEADER

The analogy of the shepherd is widespread, having developed over many thousands of years. Shepherding is one of the oldest known occupations of humanity, dating back thousands of years. Shepherding was not only lucrative in ancient cultures but became commonly associated with leadership, often because of the wealth and standing of the sheep owners. The economic value of sheep is seen in over five hundred references in the Bible as they are often owned in the many thousands, and profitable for their wool, milk, meat and obviously as a sacrificial animal in the post-exodus era.

The shepherd-leader was often seen as philanthropic, wanting the best for people and, as a result, became a symbol of leadership power and influence. Jamie Swalm explains this connection between shepherding and leadership further:

> *The shepherd leader is both benevolent, which requires humility, yet exercises significant power and authority. The simultaneous exercise of power and benevolence is at its core a paradox. Because of the universality of the image of a shepherd, the shepherd leader metaphor is a powerful vehicle through which to communicate or describe leadership principles.*[7]

The Old Testament uses the title of shepherd to describe not only those who cared for sheep but also kings and even God himself. The prophets Ezekiel and Jeremiah used the label to describe national and religious leaders, even if most of the time they were delivering a rebuke from God about the corrupt leadership they brought to the nation.

The New Testament contains sixteen different references to shepherds, and the word *pastor*, commonly used today, is the Latin word for shepherd. We see the significance across both Testaments of the identifications shepherd and pastor. Whilst we see the term shepherd in an agrarian context, we understand its adoption in the New Testament for those who would bring leadership to the church, the flock of God.

Paul uses the shepherd analogy to impress upon the leaders of the church at Ephesus the importance of their dual role, to both care for and protect the people for whom they carry responsibility:

> *Keep watch over yourselves and all the flock of which the Holy Spirit has made you overseers. Be shepherds of the church of God, which he bought with his own blood. I know that after I leave, savage wolves will come in among you and will not spare the flock.* (Acts 20:28-29)

My conviction is that shepherd-leadership is the primary form of church leadership revealed in the New Testament. It's something that encompasses much more than just a focus on caring for people. It engages the leadership skills needed to bring growth and development to a church community, or any sphere in which Christian leadership is expressed.

Among the many obvious tasks that a shepherd fulfils of caring, feeding, watering, grooming, shearing, protecting and delivering newborn lambs, is the role of leading. A shepherd directs the sheep, guiding the way they journey, just as the psalmist acknowledges in Psalm 23:3 that the Shepherd God guides us in paths of righteousness. This is the part of the shepherding responsibility I think has been subtracted and made into something impersonal and at times dictatorial, but you cannot separate it. To shepherd is to lead and to lead is to shepherd.

A MODEL OF SHEPHERD-LEADERSHIP

While shepherding's rich history spans millennia and cultures, perhaps no figure better exemplifies the transformation from shepherd to leader than Moses. His journey from tending Jethro's flocks to leading Israel illuminates the essential qualities of shepherd-leadership that remain relevant today. As we examine Moses' story, we see how God develops a shepherd's heart before entrusting his people to their care.

Born into a Hebrew family in captivity in Egypt, he is saved from the male baby massacre ordered by the pharaoh, by a loving and selfless mother. His papyrus reed basket floated down the Nile and his life changed in an instant as he was found and taken into the family of the pharaoh's daughter, though miraculously nursed through his childhood by his own mother.

Educated as an Egyptian, he learns of his Hebrew birth. In a vain attempt to protect a Hebrew slave he commits murder and flees for his life into Midian. God has his hand on Moses' life though, guiding his steps to a miraculous encounter in the desert at a burning bush. This is certainly a remarkable moment of calling, but this lost Israelite, who is shepherding his father-in-law's sheep, is called by God to lead the greatest exodus of humans in the history of the world. A forty-year journey that would stretch him to the limit. Yet his shepherd-leadership took the children of Israel to the very edge of the land that God had promised them when he spoke to Abraham hundreds of years earlier. The way that Moses led throughout the wilderness wanderings demonstrates the varying ways that a shepherd-leader must learn to lead also.

He led from among them

As the estimated 2.5 million people leave Egypt on foot, Moses, their leader, was among them. He was one of them as they escaped their captors, walked with them as they gathered what they could and headed east towards freedom in the land God had promised them. He was escaping too. He also longed for a place to call home. At this stage there were some who doubted his lineage and his credentials. That belief would come as they journeyed. Though some would still doubt him, most would follow his lead.

Relationship is something that grows as you lead from among people. Shepherd-leaders build relationships as they walk with people through all the challenges of life. We move among families and build connections with those who are single. We help the older ones in the community and laugh with the children. Can you picture Moses on the first leg of the walk to the Red Sea, becoming more part of this new community as he wanders between the tribal groups, introducing himself and learning about their life stories?

He led from in front of them

There are moments when shepherd-leaders must step up and inspire faith in those they lead. The early part of the Exodus had been trouble-free but then two great problems confronted them. One a natural obstruction, the Red Sea; the other a marauding enemy, the Egyptian army. Here Moses steps ahead of the people to declare that God will rescue them (Exodus 14:13). Imagine the confidence the Israelites had in their new leader as they look back and see the Red Sea swallow up the pursuing Egyptian army. In fact, Exodus 14:31 tells us, 'The people feared the Lord and put their trust in him and in Moses his servant.' There are moments when the leadership of the shepherd takes centre stage. Times when key decisions must be made that draw the community together and inspire steps of faith in God that revolutionise the journey that they are on together.

He led from above them

The only destination God had identified to Moses was Mount Sinai (Exodus 3:12). That was the place they were to aim for, so that they could worship God together, as a community at his holy mountain. When they arrived there, two months after leaving Egypt, Moses climbed the mountain to meet with God (Exodus 19:3). This is a shepherd-leader's primary role. Leading from above people is not a statement of power or prominence, it is fulfilling a call from God to meet with him on behalf of the community. It isn't that God doesn't speak to all his people, it's that he wants to communicate with those who are called to shepherd and lead his people, so that they will always realise that he alone is their God, and that those of us who are called to lead, do so at his instruction.

Moses typifies the connection between shepherding and leadership. His heart is always for the people he leads and he even on occasion asks God to judge him and not the people. He endures the long journey of leadership through rough terrain and the breadth of human emotions and reactions. Yet it's his faithful and loving leadership that made him a great among Israel's leaders. Moses' journey from tending Jethro's flocks to leading Israel would be echoed generations later in David's life. Both men learned the fundamentals of leadership in the fields with actual sheep before God called them to greater responsibilities. While Moses led the people to the Promised Land, David would later unite and lead them within it. Their stories, though separated by centuries, reveal consistent patterns in how God develops shepherd-leaders.

THE SHEPHERD WHO BECAME KING

During my many years in church ministry my understanding of leadership has been rooted in this biblical motif of the Shepherd-Leader. Of all the biblical characters that I believe modelled this, apart from Jesus, was David, who became King David. He stands out as one of the best examples of a shepherd-leader. There are other references to shepherds in the scriptures, but I am not only concerned with the sheep-caring role but also with the sheep-leading role. This is what I believe distinguished David as a shepherd-leader and not just a shepherd.

When we first meet him, he is only a shepherd, caring for his father's flocks. But when we see him as king of Israel, he has grown into a shepherd-leader. This journey is captured in Psalm 78:70-72:

> *He chose David his servant and took him from the sheepfolds; from tending the sheep he brought him to be the shepherd of his people Jacob, of Israel his inheritance. And David shepherded them with integrity of heart; with skilful hands he led them.*

God called David; that's what being chosen means. I focused on calling in an earlier chapter but here it is personified in David, and the truth is that David is one of the most important characters in scripture. He holds enormous significance in Jewish history and culture, and the forty years of his reign is still considered the golden era of Hebraic history. But we know that David did not start from an advantageous position. In fact, he started out hugely disadvantaged. Not chosen by his father or even the prophet Samuel, who was sent by God to anoint the king to succeed a disobedient Saul. He trained to be a shepherd. To care for his father's sheep and show genuine concern for the sheep he led. But here's the point. The care that he showed and the compassion, tenderness and attentiveness to the needs of his father's sheep required strength and courage too.

In my early years in ministry, I came across a wonderful book called *A Shepherd Looks at Psalm 23* by Phillip Keller. He spent many years as a shepherd, as well as an agrologist at the University of Toronto, and used his first-hand experience of managing sheep ranches to contextualise the most famous of all the psalms. He explains the significance of so many of the words in Psalm 23 in the light of a sheep's characteristics, habits and idiosyncrasies. But he also shines a light on ancient shepherding practices that demonstrate the skills and characteristics needed by a shepherd to rear healthy, reproductive sheep. He speaks at one point of the kind of leadership necessary in the adverse environment an ancient shepherd would have led his sheep:

> *All the dangers of rampaging rivers in flood; avalanches; rockslides; poisonous plants; the ravages of predators that raged the flock or the awesome storms of sleet and hail and snow were familiar to him. He handled the sheep and managed them with care under all these adverse conditions. Nothing took him by surprise. He was fully prepared to safeguard his flock and tend them with skill under every circumstance.*[8]

This was David's experience, and a genuine example of a shepherd-leader that encompasses far more than sitting playing his harp under a tree while the sheep mowed the fields of their grass. This becomes clearer in the account of David's confrontation with the giant from Gath, Goliath. We read about this in 1 Samuel 17, and it gives us a window not only into David's early life as a shepherd, but the man and leader he was becoming following his secretive anointing as the king to succeed Saul in his dad's back garden in Bethlehem.

He is making regular visits to the battlefield where Israel is locked in a confrontation with the Philistines – again. He takes food for his brothers and then returns to Bethlehem to help his father look after the sheep. I can't help but see the connection here between the day-to-day responsibilities of normal shepherding alongside the occasional moments when we face the giant confrontations of spiritual leadership. These moments don't come along very often but are always situations the shepherd-leader must be prepared for, as is certainly the case with young David. On that day, David experiences the cowardice of Saul's army, and even the king himself, as Goliath steps forward once more to taunt the Israelites facing him. David, the shepherd, is shocked as the Israelite army runs away in fear. This is not who he is. There is something much deeper in his faith in God's promise to fight for Israel and lead them in victory against their enemies.

That's what energises him to approach the mighty king Saul and offer himself to be the champion who will take on the giant in the name of the God of Israel. It's when Saul doubts David's capacity to fight the Philistine that we discover the warrior he has already become when protecting his father's sheep and goats.

> *When a lion or a bear came and carried off a sheep from the flock, I went after it, struck it, and rescued the sheep from its mouth. When it turned on me, I seized it by its hair, struck it and killed it. Your servant has killed both the lion and the bear; this uncircumcised Philistine will be like one of them, because he has defied the armies of the living God. The Lord who rescued me from the paw of the lion and the paw of the bear will rescue me from the hand of this Philistine.* (1 Samuel 17:34-37)

We see his courage in walking down into the Valley of Elah, armed only with his trusted sling, having refused the grand armour of the king to protect him. We see his conviction as he defiantly ignores the threats of Goliath and confronts him in the name of the Lord Almighty. We see his confidence as he tells Goliath what is about to happen to all nine-feet-nine-inches of him. But we also see his calmness as he takes one of the five stones he had collected from the stream on his way down the valley, places it in his shepherd's sling, and hits Goliath right in the middle of his forehead.

The lesson I want to draw from this popular moment in David's life is that it was his shepherd's skill that enabled him to defeat the giant that others feared, and not any military prowess or equipment. Shepherd-leadership requires all those characteristics I identified in David. Courage, conviction, confidence and calmness. Loving and leading people is the most demanding and stretching thing I have done in my life. I have needed courage on many occasions and at other times needed to stand firmly on the convictions I have in God and his word. Some days I have lacked confidence and on other days I have felt the stirring of the Spirit to step forward and make big decisions or confront big challenges. These are not any different for all shepherd-leaders. A shepherd-leader learns to face giants and stand them down, just as David did. It's not simply about being nice to people; it's about protecting them. And when they have wandered into dangerous places or been ensnared by threatening enemies, it's having the courage to step in and rescue them.

THE LEADERS WHO SHEPHERD

While David's reign ended three millennia ago, the principles of shepherd-leadership he embodied remain powerfully relevant today. As modern church leaders navigate the complexities of twenty-first century ministry, David's integration of tender care and strong leadership offers a timeless model. I witnessed this same dynamic in my own ministry journey, particularly during my transformative experience with Jack Hayford, a contemporary example of shepherding God's people with both 'integrity of heart' and 'skilful hands'.

To many in North America he was known as the Pastor's Pastor. He was a theologian with a heart for people and a passion for the local church. He excelled in many spheres of ministry and over decades saw an amazing move of God at The Church on the Way in Van Nuys, Los Angeles. In 2004 I had the amazing opportunity to spend five days at his School of Pastoral Nurture. I was the only person from the UK at this event at which there were forty other pastors. It was specifically designed to be a small classroom environment, and I got the joy of mixing with local church pastors from the USA, Canada but also South Africa.

In that setting hosted at the King's Seminary, which was then sited in Van Nuys, we sat for five days being taught by Pastor Jack through the book of

Ephesians. His primary focus was all about loving and leading God's people in the context of the local church. It was an extraordinary and impactful time. But the highlight was the Friday evening when we were all invited to Pastor Jack's house for supper. His wife prepared some wonderful food, and we freely roamed around his home relaxing in this modest, yet comfortable, family environment with Pastor Jack and Annie. He invited a professional singer to come and entertain us in his lounge. He mingled with us, laughed with us, showed us his den filled with family photos and a few special ones with presidents and celebrities. But he taught us more in those few hours about being concerned for people and the humility that had been so central to his life and ministry than we had learned even in the excellence of what we were taught in the classroom. I could see close-up why he was called the Pastor's Pastor.

I love how Jack Hayford always represented the significance of shepherd-leadership. In his book *Pastors of Promise* he writes:

> *The Almighty holds shepherds in very high regard, and His Word reveals sheep tending as a high-level office in heaven's books. It shows the role of shepherding as being filled with significance – to be defined and rewarded on the highest terms.*[9]

Shepherd-leaders don't abandon vision, strategy and leadership. These things are critical to providing direction and guidance to any community. The church is called to advance and to win the lost, to grow as a community and to lovingly influence our towns and cities. But authentic shepherd-leaders keep people as the motivating factor in all that they are seeking to lead. They stir passion and dreams for what can be. They use their skills to develop plans for how these aspirations can be achieved. They raise the levels of people's faith to believe that God is with us, for us, and ahead of us in every great exploit. But they love those they lead, and they are considerate and never seek to manipulate or coerce people purely for their own benefit.

This is why I love those verses I quoted earlier from Psalm 78, and specifically the final little sentence: 'David shepherded them with integrity of heart; with skilful hands he led them.' This description simply defines the relationship between shepherding and leadership. It identifies that integrity and skill are compatible, and heart and ability can be powerful twins. This verse reminds me regularly that I can grow my leadership skills and ability, but I can also learn more about how to love people and maintain a purity in my heart that pleases the Lord. This is how I would love my own ministry to be remembered when I'm singing along with the celestial choir in the eternal kingdom.

Those words, spoken about David, don't tell the full story of his life and leadership. Whilst he was described as a man after God's own heart, his imperfections are recorded for us to read as much as his triumphs. His behaviour towards Bathsheba was inexcusable, and his subtle murder of her husband Uriah was worthy of the death penalty if he hadn't hidden behind his powerful role as the king. So, I don't want to paint a picture of David that is hiding his weaknesses and sins. I will say more about this episode in David's life in a later chapter. But I hope that we can see in the way that he led, something that can stir a desire in us to be women and men who excel as leaders because people know they are loved as much as they are being led with vision and faith.

Shepherds lead reluctant sheep where they may not be sure about going. From pastures that have been exhausted to fields that are fresh and new. They lead them away from dangers they can't see and towards opportunities they haven't imagined. A shepherd-leader is a critically important responsibility in the body of Christ. It needs to be taken up by men and women who are totally committed to building safe and loving communities, where lost people can find Jesus and the kind of healing they need from the devastating effects of our broken world. In these communities they can be encouraged to discover the greatest purpose of all, which is to use their gifts and talents to work in partnership with the Holy Spirit in extending God's kingdom into every part of our culture.

Now that takes real leadership. But it also takes great care. It requires women and men who would aspire to lead and yet be driven by love. It asks those who long to preach to crowds to also get on their faces in prayer before God for those who sit and listen to what they have to say every week. It means we will lay our lives down for the sheep that God has entrusted to our care and not ask them to make every sacrifice imaginable so that the shepherd can live in greater comfort or opulence.

This is, for me, the heart of biblical leadership, and certainly leadership in the local church. I fear, at times, it is the kind of leadership that we have strayed from and reaped all kinds of problems as a result. There are no perfect shepherd-leaders, and I know I'm not one either. But I hope we can hunger afresh to be leaders who can balance well these dual aspects appropriately. To lead with courage and conviction but to watch over the flock that the Lord himself has given us responsibility for. After all, they are his sheep not ours. And the Good Shepherd has every right to hold us accountable for the way that we lead them.

AN ANCIENT JOB DESCRIPTION

The most powerful leadership model in history begins with an unexpected metaphor: the shepherd. It's a paradox that challenges our modern sensibilities – how could the mundane task of herding animals become the divine pattern for spiritual leadership? Yet this is precisely what God chose as his primary metaphor for leadership, a choice that carries profound implications for how we lead his people today.

This ancient model stands in stark contrast to contemporary pastoral job descriptions. A quick online search reveals requirements that would have been unimaginable a generation ago: expertise in safeguarding protocols, proficiency in digital communication, mastery of organisational management, and more. While these modern competencies are essential – particularly critical issues like safeguarding in the twenty-first century – they can sometimes overshadow the fundamental nature of spiritual leadership that God established through the shepherd metaphor.

What if we could bridge this gap between ancient wisdom and modern demands? What if we could discover a leadership framework that not only remains compatible with today's challenges but also equips us to model the character of the Shepherd God? Such a framework exists in perhaps the most familiar passage of scripture – Psalm 23. This poetic text, penned by a young shepherd boy while tending his father's flock, offers more than comfort to troubled souls; it provides a timeless blueprint for leadership that can transform how we guide God's people in every age.

When we examine this ancient text through the lens of leadership, we discover something profound about the nature of God himself –

for throughout scripture God reveals himself primarily through two relational metaphors that illuminate his leadership: he is both the Father of his children and the Shepherd of his sheep. These twin images appear consistently, whether describing his relationship with ancient Israel or the New Testament church. As Philip Keller observes:

> *These concepts were first conceived in the mind of God ... so when the simple – though sublime – statement is made by a man or a woman that 'the Lord is my shepherd', it immediately implies a profound yet practical working relationship between a human being and his maker.*[10]

This divine pattern forms the foundation for all biblical leadership, and by extension, all leadership in the contemporary Christian church. We don't have the luxury of creating our own leadership models. As beings created in God's image, we are called to both love and lead in ways that reflect his character. Frank Damazio captures this imperative perfectly: 'The heart of the shepherd is the closest thing to the heart of God for His church. The Christian leader must do more than understand it – he or she must live it.'[11]

Both the Father and Shepherd metaphors speak to deeply caring relationships. In each role, the leader puts the needs of others – whether children or sheep – before their own interests. While their wisdom and knowledge far exceed that of those in their care, they lead with grace and understanding. Sometimes this means making decisions that their charges cannot yet comprehend – but this is precisely what good fathers and shepherds do. They both love and lead, a dual calling we see perfectly expressed in the Shepherd God.

We might be tempted to romanticise the shepherd metaphor, but David's experience tells a different story. For him, shepherding was a demanding and often dangerous occupation that required constant vigilance. He carried significant responsibility for his family's livelihood – the quality of the wool, milk and meat depended entirely on his care and management. As some have noted, 'David's poem about shepherd-leadership might seem more relevant to twenty-first-century business leaders'[12] than we might initially expect.

THE SHEPHERD-LEADER'S PROFILE

This brings us to Psalm 23 – not just as a source of comfort, but as an ancient job description for those who aspire to lead God's people. What follows is an exploration of how this timeless text can shape a contemporary leadership profile, one that bridges the gap between ancient wisdom and modern demands.

The Shepherd provides resources

'The Lord is my shepherd, I lack nothing. He makes me lie down in green pastures, he leads me beside quiet waters' . . .

- Ensuring their followers have all necessary resources to thrive and succeed
- Creates an environment of abundance rather than scarcity
- Anticipates needs before they become critical shortages

The shepherd role requires attentiveness to the needs of those they lead. All living creatures have basic needs. The need for food, water and shelter, and the same applies to the spiritual needs of disciples of Jesus. Jesus' instruction to Peter is clear enough for all of us, 'Feed my lambs' (John 21:15). Ancient shepherds, in semi-arid environments, had to labour hard to create pasture for their sheep. This required skills in clearing land and seeding the soil so that crops of forage could feed the flock. Similarly, they would know how to locate pools of water or even build wells they could lead the sheep to.

The task of nourishing the sheep is still the task of shepherd-leaders. Phil Pringle talks about setting aside a day and a half each week to prepare what he would share with the church on Sundays. He explains: 'Feeding the flock is the top priority for any pastor. If a pastor is too busy for that, then that pastor is simply too busy. We must all attend to our primary calling more fully.'[13]

This commitment to feed and nourish the flock extends beyond Sunday sermons to other moments and opportunities to teach people how they can prioritise the feeding of their souls. The resources available to the modern follower of Jesus are extraordinary compared with our forefathers. There is small-group curriculum, digital Bible-study tools, guided journals and a library of excellent commentaries and devotional reading for believers at all stages of their spiritual journey. The very best preaching and teaching should inspire a hunger in people's souls to search the scriptures themselves, growing and deepening their spiritual life as they feed on the word with the help of the Spirit.

The Shepherd promotes wellness

'He refreshes my soul' . . .

- Prioritises the wellbeing of people over the success of programmes
- Recognises the signs of stress and difficulty and proactively addresses them
- Creates opportunities for renewal and restoration

There is something beautiful in David's words here that should still shape the heart of shepherd-leadership. They recognise how fragile the human condition can be, and how much we need help outside of ourselves. Phillip Keller shares his experience, as a shepherd, of *restoring* cast sheep. A cast sheep was one which had lain down comfortably in a sunken area and when it tried to move was unable to get up as its centre of gravity had moved. This left the sheep on its back with its feet in the air, and in a state of panic. Keller explains how he would begin to *restore* the sheep:

> *Tenderly I would roll the sheep over on its side. This would relieve the pressure of gases in the rumen. If she had been*

down for long, I would have to lift her onto her feet. Then, straddling the sheep with my legs, I would hold her erect, rubbing her limbs to restore the circulation to her legs. This often took quite a little time. When the sheep started to walk again, she often just stumbled, staggered, and collapsed in a heap once more . . . Little by little the sheep would regain its equilibrium. It would start to walk steadily and surely. By and by it would dash away to rejoin the others, set free from its fears and frustrations, given another chance to live a little longer.[14]

How many times have we been called to assist those who cannot help themselves? It may be the case that they have been there before, but the shepherd-leader once more tenderly helps their immobilised soul find equilibrium and the ability to walk on. The wellbeing of those we lead will always be of the utmost importance and something that can't simply be delegated. Whilst this level of individual care is not always possible in some larger settings, the emphasis on healing and renewal comes from the shepherd with primary responsibility for the spiritual family.

At the heart of genuine shepherd-leadership is the deep desire for people to know a contentment in their soul. This is where specific thought and planning into the kind of ministry that will bring healing for the wounds that people are so often carrying can revitalise their lives with fresh hope, and peace should be high on the agenda of leadership or eldership team meetings.

The Shepherd leads by example

'He guides me along the right paths for his name's sake' . . .

- Models a focus on ethical and righteous living
- Maps clear pathways for growth and development
- Aligns people with the character of Christ

Newer translations of the Bible have changed familiar words in this psalm that many of us grew up knowing. One of those changes takes something away from the significance of the way the shepherd leads. To say that the shepherd guides may not seem too different. But I cannot help but feel it reduces the importance of leadership in ethical and righteous living.

The greatest lessons a shepherd gives are found in how they live, not how they preach. Too many leaders think they can lead people with persuasive or erudite words, when in fact it is character that people follow not oratory. John Maxwell describes character as more than talk. He says, 'Anyone can say that he has integrity, but action is the real indicator of character. Your character determines who you are. Who you are determines what you see. What you see determines what you do. That's why you can never separate a leader's character from his actions.'[15] Shepherds lead in those pathways of goodness as they walk them too.

The Shepherd navigates crisis

'Even though I walk through the darkest valley, I will fear no evil, for you are with me; your rod and your staff, they comfort me' . . .

- Remains present and composed during painful situations
- Provides steady guidance through difficult choices
- Shields the flock from unnecessary stress and anxiety

The valleys are always the hardest places to walk in life. Everybody experiences them. They are the negative and difficult seasons of life that are found in things such as bereavement, divorce, sickness, unemployment, depression and a host of human moments that seem impossible to exit. The shepherd-leader is one who is present, you are a *there* person. When people are restless, anxious and fearful you provide a stable and supporting presence.

I was so overwhelmed with joy when I looked across the congregation just as I shared the gospel appeal. It is thrilling whenever someone lifts their hand to signal their desire to take the next step of surrendering their life to Jesus. But when that is someone who you have been earnestly praying for, it's even more exciting. This particular night, Ron raised his hand. But not just Ron, his son-in-law Mick did too. We had been praying for Ron and Mick for quite a while. Ever since Ron's wife Sheila and his daughter Karen had made the same decision to follow Jesus.

Ron was well into his retirement years by now and became one of those people it's just so easy to love. A gentle man who was honest and sincere in all that he did, which included lovingly playing Father Christmas for a number of years at the mums-and-toddlers Christmas party. But eventually Ron's health began to fail him and in October 2010 he was admitted to hospital and became seriously ill.

I can vividly remember the day in October when Mick called me to say that the doctors were quite sure that Ron only had a brief time to live. Amanda and the children were away during the half-term break at her mum's in Wales and I had made my usual bangers and mash for dinner. As I took Mick's call, I was taking my first morsel of this culinary delight but said I would get to the hospital as soon as I could.

I arrived in the ward no more than thirty minutes later and was taken behind the curtains drawn around Ron's bed. Sheila, Karen, Mick and Ron's grandson Andrew were there. This was such a beautifully tight-knit family we all loved in our church. At this moment, though, they were agonising over the prospect of Ron's departure from them. To be invited into a deeply personal and sensitive moment such as this, with a family I loved, was a huge privilege. The trust they had put in me to help them navigate the moment of loss they were about to engage with, is still etched in my memory. It was obvious that we were at the very last moments of Ron's earthly journey. But what was obvious, too, was that we were not without hope and comfort because of that decision to follow Jesus he had made a decade or so earlier.

It's not always clear what to do in such a moment, but I remember asking Sheila, 'Are you ready for him to go home?' She responded with a gentle nod, which belied the huge sacrifice this was for her after over sixty years of marriage together. We held hands and I quoted Psalm 23. I prayed, and we all seemed to know instinctively that Ron had just peacefully slipped from this life into his eternal inheritance. I cannot describe what that felt like. The combination of sadness for Sheila and her family, but also the enormity of watching someone who I had seen surrender his life to Jesus step into the unimaginable reward that decision brings. I was overwhelmed, and still am when I think about that moment.

I don't say this lightly when I tell you I cannot think of a more moving and powerful moment in all my decades of ministry. I've preached to crowds and conducted many special occasions, but that moment will live with me forever. This is what shepherd-leaders do. They walk with people through their darkest and saddest moments, but they realise what an honour it is to be there.

The Shepherd resolves conflict

'You prepare a table before me in the presence of my enemies'...

- Addresses opposition and challenges with wisdom
- Creates safe spaces for difficult conversations
- Mediates conflict whilst maintaining relationships

Many leaders fear the possibility of conflict, hoping they can avoid it at all costs. Yet conflict is part of life. It's unavoidable and requires shepherd-leaders who won't run away from it, or reactively run towards it, but who will take the necessary steps to respond thoughtfully and proportionally to moments of disagreement and difficulty. Sheep may seem quite peaceful creatures, but they have moments of intense rivalry too. This happens most notably during the mating season when there is a fight for the attention of the ewes. This kind of pecking order is as old as creation itself and not confined just to the sheep population. In many churches similar pecking orders see people vying for influence and attention, and petty squabbles can end up in all-out wars.

Shepherd-leaders create the environment where disagreements can be resolved with both truth and grace. When this isn't possible the shepherd-leader must step in and seek to resolve conflict in the most righteous way possible, and at the very least protect the peace of the flock.

The Shepherd inspires joy

'You anoint my head with oil; my cup overflows'...

- Invites people into the life of the Spirit
- Guards both team and congregation from burnout
- Celebrates moments of wonder and delight

I wonder sometimes whether it's just the power of hindsight or the snare of nostalgia that I can remember more of the wonderful moments of leading a local church, than I can the difficult ones. Whatever it is, I'm glad I can. Because that is what church has the power to be and shepherding people should, in the main, be a joyous experience. The Spirit comes to each of us to bring life, fullness of life. Leading people to experience his blessing is a vital focus for the shepherd-leader.

Leadership is about developing a climate where people can flourish and not be burned out with activity. I fear that too many churches are too busy. Often foliage is mistaken for fruit. Lots of activity in the church can be nothing more than leaves on a tree. Joy is not found in advertising how much our church does, but in how much our people are thriving in life.

How much they are exuding the fruit of the Spirit and enjoying the delight of serving Jesus. Good shepherd-leaders understand how to celebrate the right things, the things that are prompted by the Spirit.

The Shepherd builds culture

'Surely your goodness and love will follow me all the days of my life'...

- Establishes an atmosphere of welcome and belonging
- Practises loving leadership in all their interactions
- Creates lasting positive impact on all those in the church family

People prosper best in an environment of goodness and kindness. We have learned more over recent years about the importance of atmospheres in our churches where people feel they can belong. Places where their lives are enriched by how people behave and interact with one another. This is what we call culture, and shepherd-leaders are the primary builders of what this looks like.

The shepherd-leader's role in culture-building operates on three distinct levels. First, there's the visible level – the way we structure our gatherings, handle newcomers and facilitate connections. Second, there's the behavioural level – how we model and reinforce values like authenticity, grace and mutual care. Finally, there's the deeper level of underlying beliefs – the shared convictions about God's nature, human worth and community that shape everything else.

Jesus exemplified this culture-building in how he developed his disciples. He didn't just teach them; he created an environment where they could fail safely, ask honest questions and gradually transform. This same pattern should mark our leadership. When people enter our churches, they should encounter not just programmes but a palpable atmosphere of God's goodness and love.

We have learned from the Parable of the Sower in Matthew chapter 13, that it is not the quality of the seed that determines fruitfulness, but the quality of the soil. The seed was the same wherever it fell. However, the quality of the place it landed determined how fruitful the seed became. Similarly, while the kingdom of God doesn't change according to location or congregation, how it's received depends greatly on the cultural soil we cultivate. This is why shepherd-leaders should prioritise the culture and ask themselves honestly if they are responsible in any way for an environment that stunts growth or encourages it.

The Shepherd creates expectation

'And I will dwell in the house of the LORD forever'...

- Inspires a love for the presence of God
- Maintains focus on eternal perspectives
- Reproduces hope-centred leadership

People want to be where the presence of God is. This declaration by the psalmist has both a current and an eternal perspective. It reflects the beauty of God's presence now and the hope of his presence to come. This is the paradox that we live in. The *house of the Lord* is not referring to the buildings we meet in, but the people we are and the presence of God among us. This place we long for has nothing to do with worship styles or ecclesiological structures. At times people have foolishly been taught that God prefers the modern over the ancient, or vice versa. It's nonsense. God loves worship in a cathedral and in a concert hall, as long as it's worship in 'Spirit and in truth' (John 4:24).

As shepherd-leaders we are called to lead people to long for the presence of God, and to learn that we are each his dwelling (1 Corinthians 3:16). But to also long for what is to come. For that moment we will see him face to face. People need hope and nothing inspires hope more than to know with confidence that this life cannot steal from us what Christ has won for us.

WALKING THE ANCIENT PATH

When David penned Psalm 23, he wasn't writing a leadership manual – he was describing his intimate experience of being led by God. Yet in doing so, he captured something profound about the nature of spiritual leadership that remains vitally relevant today. Like stones in a path worn smooth by countless feet, these principles have proven their worth across millennia of church leadership.

The essentials of shepherd-leadership aren't found in the modern trappings of church administration or the latest leadership theories, valuable as these may be. They're found in the timeless tasks of providing, protecting, guiding, healing and nurturing. A shepherd-leader ensures their people are fed spiritually, creates safe spaces for growth, models righteous living, walks with them through dark valleys, mediates conflicts, cultivates joy, builds healthy cultures and keeps their gaze fixed on eternal perspectives.

These responsibilities haven't changed since David's time because human needs haven't changed. People still need leaders who will put their welfare first, who will be present in a crisis, who will create environments where they can flourish, and who will point them towards God's presence. The shepherd model reminds us that leadership isn't primarily about position or power – it's about presence and service.

As we face the complex challenges of leading God's people in the twenty-first century, the ancient pattern of shepherd-leadership offers us not just a metaphor, but a proven path forward. When we embrace these principles, we find ourselves walking in the footsteps of the Shepherd God, participating in a leadership model that God himself designed and demonstrates. In doing so, the mundane task of shepherding becomes something sacred – a living expression of divine love in action.

5
THE SHEEP ARE IN DANGER

On 24th August 2012 a Lancashire court heard a shocking case of modern sheep rustling. A shepherd had stolen £15,000 worth of sheep from a neighbouring farm, only to be caught when DNA evidence matched the stolen animals to their original flock. What made this crime particularly disturbing wasn't just its contemporary setting, but that these sheep were stolen by another shepherd – someone meant to protect, not prey upon, the flock.

This incident serves as a powerful metaphor for the dangers facing God's people today. Just as those sheep were betrayed by one who should have been their protector, the church faces threats not only from outside its walls but sometimes from within its own leadership structures. When Paul wrote to the Ephesians about Christ giving 'pastors' to the church (Ephesians 4:11), he understood that God's people need genuine shepherds precisely because the journey of faith is fraught with danger. While persecution remains a stark reality for many Christians worldwide, Western believers face more subtle but equally serious threats to their spiritual wellbeing – including the devastating impact of compromised leadership.

Jesus addressed the dangers for his followers in the explanation of himself as the Good Shepherd. We find this teaching in John chapter 10 but need to be careful we don't overlook the context for what Jesus describes in John 10:1: 'Very truly I tell you Pharisees, anyone who does not enter the sheepfold by the gate, but climbs in by some other way, is a thief and a robber.'

This opening phrase is important: 'Very truly I tell you Pharisees'. Jesus is pointing the finger at the Pharisees whose aim it is to destroy the impact of his remarkable ministry on the broken and needy people of Israel. He identifies them as a huge part of the danger for his sheep, his followers.

The Pharisees are desperate to maintain their own positions of power and privilege and refuse to rejoice in the healing of a man born blind, or any other miracle that flowed from Jesus. They are a danger to the sheep he has come to save and heal and do not carry concern for the wellbeing of the people they claim to lead with spiritual authority. Here Jesus models something very different to the Pharisees, but also to us as Christian leaders. It's a distressing thought that those who are in a position to care for and protect the people of God can pose a great risk to them. As we will see below, this had been a problem before we read of the Pharisees in the New Testament, and sadly remains a problem in some parts of the Christian church today.

Using the metaphor of sheep in this passage is intentional for Jesus. Throughout his teaching he has in mind the vulnerability of this breed of animal. Sheep, one of the oldest domesticated animals, have been bred for their wool, meat and milk for thousands of years. They are gentle and docile creatures, but unfortunately, they are also vulnerable to a variety of predators that threaten their survival. Predators also cause significant stress for sheep. Even if a predator doesn't kill any sheep, their presence can cause fear and anxiety in the flock. This can lead to a range of problems, including reduced weight gain, lower fertility and decreased milk production.

The specific dangers for those early followers of Jesus were in many ways very different from what they are for many of us today, but at the same time there are some that are universal for all ages of God's children. Though Jesus clearly points a finger at the Pharisees in these words, there can be no doubt he is also referring to a far more dangerous threat, a spiritual threat. That spiritual threat Jesus identifies as the thief. This thief is the same enemy who confronted Jesus in the Judean wilderness at the beginning of his ministry. The one who pursued Jesus throughout his journey to the cross and undoubtedly taunted him in Gethsemane as Jesus agonised over what was ahead of him. Warren Wiersbe has summarised well the dangerous intent of the devil, the thief:

> *Satan's thievery extends beyond the individual to the church as a whole. He seeks to rob us of unity, of sound doctrine, and of our first love for Christ. His danger lies in his ability to make his deceptions appear as light.*[16]

Naturally, we are cautious about placing too much emphasis on the works of Satan, but at the same time we cannot ignore his commitment to destroy the devotion of God's children. This is Lucifer, the former archangel, who was cast from heaven in eternity past for leading a rebellion against God. Here, Jesus reminds us that this rebellion continues to wage against those who choose to follow him, and that shepherd-leaders are called to offer protection, comfort, support and strength to his people as they live their lives of faith.

WARNING THE SHEEP

As I reflect on the many privileged years of leading people, I can recall many occasions when it was necessary to warn some of the dangers that they were facing with decisions they were about to make or steps they were clearly considering taking.

I vividly remember sitting with a couple whose marriage had been acrimonious for several years, and who were clearly at a crossroads as I was asked to intervene in the conflict that had flared up between them. We met in a lounge area in our church offices. He sat on a sofa at one end, she a sofa at the other, and I sat uncomfortably between the two of them like a rugby referee about to engage a scrum down. The tension was palpable, and it felt like both had come armed with their arguments and justifications for their attitudes and actions of late. In that moment I could only think of the three children they had brought up who would be innocent victims in this ensuing battle.

I didn't hold back in politely warning them that this was a moment to pause and ask what life might be like for those dear children if they, two grown adults, did not consider their next steps and invite the Lord to guide them. I think I knew at the time that my words fell on deaf ears, and the events that unfolded over the next decade proved it. The family broke apart, causing huge pain to both adults and all three children, who were pulled and pushed by their Christian parents to be loyal to one or the other.

These are the kinds of dangers, among many others, that shepherd-leaders warn against. They are dangers that our enemy ensures befall all of us. He is not for one second concerned about our feelings. In fact, it is quite the opposite. He is actively pursuing an agenda aimed at destroying the devotion of God's people. All shepherd-leaders need to grow in discernment to enable them to see the signs of the enemy's strategies at work. This doesn't always happen as a direct demonic attack; in fact, it's my view that this happens less than some suggest. But whenever God's children are experiencing loss and pain, they are discovering how the thief seeks to break in and steal the peace and joy that the Good Shepherd promises.

LEADING TO SAFETY

It is not just the responsibility of the shepherd-leader to warn of ever-present danger, but also to lead those who follow them to places of safety, peace and joy. This is the beautiful contrast to the dangers that stand in the way. Though the journey of following Jesus is fraught with dangers it is also filled with incredible joy.

As Jesus prepares for his ascension, he creates an opportunity to call the less than perfect Peter to be a shepherd-leader of his people. Yes, Peter who denied even knowing Jesus. What a reminder that no shepherd-leader is perfect – far from it. This conversation between Jesus and Peter has often been focused on to illustrate Peter's recovery after his denial of Jesus, and that is certainly a major part of the conversation. But let's not forget what Jesus instructs Peter to prioritise.

In John 21:15-17 Jesus asks Peter three times if he loves him. But three times he also identifies what he wants Peter to do. Twice he tells him 'Feed my sheep' and once 'Take care of my lambs'. No word came from the mouth of Jesus unintentionally. Everything he said carried weight and purpose. Peter is given a clear message: he is saying 'my sheep matter', take care of them.

But this New Testament account does not stand alone when it comes to identifying what good shepherd-leadership looks like, in contrast to bad leadership, or dare I say it, dangerous leadership.

REBUKING THE BAD SHEPHERDS

In Ezekiel 34 Yahweh speaks through the prophet to challenge the leadership of Israel, who he, God, identified as shepherds. They were the magistrates, the priests and Levites, the great Sanhedrin or council of state, those who had the direction of public affairs in a higher or lower sphere. These leaders, who God had charged to lead the nation well, were in God's mind responsible for the wellbeing of the people. The nation, after all, was not defined by its institutions, but its people.

The passage concerns leadership. Kings are equated to shepherds. These rulers had exploited the people as if the flock belonged to them. But the people were the Lord's, and the kings ruled over them by the Lord's appointment. Ezekiel 34:1-10 describes the horrendous behaviour of these shepherds. They exploited the people by taking the best of the food and the wool for clothing. They have also shown no concern or compassion for the weak, the sick, the injured, the strays or the lost, and they ruled harshly and with brutality

The rebuke given to these shepherds was significant. They were guilty of negligence, exploitation, greed and indifference. They were accused by God as those 'who take care only of yourselves' and those who 'eat the curds, clothe yourselves with the wool and slaughter the choice animals, but you do not take care of the flock of God'. They are making sure they eat the finest foods and wear the finest clothes, even if this means the strongest sheep in the flock must die.

The principle that Jesus models is the exact opposite: 'I am the good shepherd. The good shepherd lays down his life for the sheep' (John 10:11). Sadly, there are some leaders today who expect the sheep to lay down their life for the shepherd. Their pursuit of privilege has been at the expense of the sheep. In some extreme cases pastors and preachers have quite literally fleeced the flock.

This is not an easy section for me to write. I really wanted my book to focus on the positive and life-giving attributes of shepherd-leadership and to celebrate the countless men and women who love their flock so much they consistently make personal sacrifices of their time, finances and energies to care for and protect those God has given them to lead. Yet I also know it is important to highlight at least some of the dangerous behaviours and expectations of a minority of Christian leaders in the hope that we can establish better models and values for shepherd-leadership. There are some parallels with the bad shepherds of Ezekiel 34 that we must beware of.

The rebuke God delivered through Ezekiel to Israel's shepherds reverberates through the centuries to challenge church leadership today. While the specific context has changed from ancient Israel to modern ministry, the core issues remain startlingly relevant. The self-serving shepherds who exploited God's flock in Ezekiel's time find their modern counterparts in leadership behaviours that still endanger the church. Just as God confronted specific failures of Israel's shepherds – their negligence, exploitation and harsh rule – we must examine how these same fundamental problems manifest in contemporary church leadership.

While most pastors and Christian leaders serve faithfully, recent decades have revealed patterns of leadership that echo the very behaviours God condemned through his prophet. These patterns typically emerge in three distinct ways: through ambitious leaders who prioritise personal success over serving the flock, absent leaders who fail to provide genuine care and presence, and, most seriously, abusive leaders who harm those entrusted to their care.

Ambitious leaders

Ambition of itself is not necessarily wrong. In fact, you could say that the gospel itself is aspirational. It allows men and women to believe that their life can be something more than they ever dreamed of. In many careers and professions, it is expected that you will have the desire to succeed and climb the corporate ladder. But there is no such ladder when it comes to Christian service. In fact, as we will see in a later chapter, greatness in God's kingdom is not upward but downwards. It's being willing to get on your knees and wash feet – the epitome of service. When leaders aspire only for their own fruitfulness and success (whatever definition you might use) then they can pose a danger to those they have been positioned to serve.

I must be honest here. In my very early years in ministry, I was ambitious. Well, at the very least, I wanted to lead a large church, preach to huge crowds and find recognition in the denomination that I was called to serve. I thought politically when it came to the denomination and loved to engage in conversation about how things could be better and how our leaders should be creating change. It doesn't sound much, but it was, at times, a negative preoccupation. I'm thankful that over many years I learned how fruitless such desires really were. I was called to love and lead people and that is the greatest thrill and satisfaction. It just took me a little longer than it should have done to realise the fruitlessness of such pursuits.

When a shepherd-leader's ambitions are primarily for the people that they lead they have found a great place. When we long for them to know God deeply and experience his life-changing presence closely, we find our ambitions aligned with his. St Richard was Bishop of Chichester in the mid-thirteenth century and prayed a pray that was, in part, made famous in the 1970s by the musical *Godspell*. The full original prayer said this:

> *Thanks be to thee, my Lord Jesus Christ,*
> *for all the benefits thou hast given me,*
> *for all the pains and insults thou hast borne for me.*
> *O most merciful redeemer, friend and brother,*
> *may I know thee more clearly,*
> *love thee more dearly,*
> *and follow thee more nearly, day by day.*
> *Amen.*

It's so important that shepherd-leaders do not see those they lead as the vehicle for their own aspirations. The greatest rewards in ministry are never our own achievements. Rather, they are seeing those we lead growing and thriving in their lives and walk with God. This is the fruit that lasts, the fruit that will reproduce itself in others.

Absent leaders

Amanda and I have been blessed with three wonderful children, and we're also grandparents. I remember my mum telling me that she never thought she could love anybody as much as she loved her children, and then her grandchildren came along. I now know exactly what she meant. We adore our grandchildren and, now and again, we get the joy of looking after them when my son and daughter-in-law take a well-earned night out or even a few days away.

As tiring as it can be – after all, neither of us are spring chickens anymore – we do all we can to ensure the children are safe, well fed (even with too many sugary Grampa treats) and have a lot of fun. It's special knowing that my son and his wife trust us to care for their precious children. We would never put the TV on, or put them to bed and just go out, leaving them on their own. Let's be honest, even in *Home Alone* poor Kevin is left by accident and not with any deliberate intent by his family. Why would Father God trust his children to shepherd-leaders who would absent themselves from their duty of care?

The first minister I was assistant to, Denis Phillips, taught me that loving and leading your people is the bread and butter of leadership. He meant that the responsibilities for the church to which you have been assigned always come first. They are God's people, and all other pursuits must come second to loving them, feeding them, protecting them and inspiring them to follow Jesus, something I watched him do faithfully.

To be honest some pastors can be present in the building but absent from relationship. At times I have heard some excuse their distance from the people with some inflated idea of their own importance. They cite the size of the church as a reason for being unable to connect with the *people* and the need for them to focus more on the vision and the leadership structures.

Sheep are prone to wander. They drift very easily from the gaze of the shepherd and find themselves on the fringes of the flock, a place that increases the risk of attack from a prowling predator. The image of an Eastern shepherd walking ahead of the flock is commonplace to us today. But that doesn't for one moment suggest that such a shepherd is not aware of where their sheep are, how many are in the flock and if any have somehow gone missing. Jesus' famous parable of the lost sheep is illustration enough that God, the Shepherd, watches over his flock and is aware of where every single one of us is.

Eugene H. Peterson, who always championed shepherd-leadership, wrote:

> *The tragedy of absent leadership is the slow decay it allows within the church. Like a garden left untended, weeds of discord and error creep in, choking out the life and vitality of the congregation. Leaders who fail to actively guide and nurture their flock are failing in their most fundamental duty.*[17]

However a church or ministry may be organised to ensure that its people are cared for pastorally, no leader can absent themselves from the divine responsibility to ensure that, in any environment they have been given leadership, they are present with people and not secluded in an ivory tower of self-importance.

Abusive leaders

This is particularly difficult to write because we have seen a distressing increase in the number of leaders who have been accused of behaviours considered abusive. We know that this is not a new problem, it is a new diagnosis. The positive changes in our cultural understanding have given victims of abuse in society a voice that is listened to more frequently, and, as a result, a confidence to speak up. There are no excuses for leadership styles that oppress people or treat them in a way that damages their mental, emotional, spiritual or physical health.

This book is obviously not focused primarily on this theme as that would require far more knowledgeable contribution than I can give. But neither can we ignore the necessary identification of this problem that has emerged in churches of all sizes, denominations and styles. As Diane Langberg wrote: 'Abusive church leadership creates a toxic environment that distorts the gospel and drives people away from Christ rather than towards Him. It's a perversion of the shepherd's role from protector to predator, and it leaves deep scars on the souls of its victims.'[18]

In all styles and denominations of churches across the Western world there is an increasing awareness that toxic church environments do exist, and that they are damaging people who are caught in the vortex of pain and confusion. The rebuke of the *shepherds of Israel* six hundred years before Christ came illustrates that God sees the effects of abusive leadership. Though the language of the Old Testament would be considered antiquated by our modern vocabulary, we can easily see the parallels, but also the heart of God for those injured and broken. He expresses his compassionate intent clearly:

> *I myself will tend my sheep and have them lie down, declares the Sovereign LORD. I will search for the lost and bring back the strays. I will bind up the injured and strengthen the weak, but the sleek and the strong I will destroy. I will shepherd the flock with justice.* (Ezekiel 34:15-16)

We should continue to challenge forms of leadership that damage people and do not focus on bringing hope and healing to them. All these types of leaders present a danger to God's children. Leadership has become attractive to many who aspire for recognition and popularity. But beware that you do not fail to hear the call of the Good Shepherd, 'Take care of my sheep.'

Will he ask us when we meet him face to face if our following on social media was huge or if we had thousands of views of our sermons on YouTube? I doubt it. Will he ask us if we protected those we were entrusted to lead? I won't be surprised if he does.

6
LEADING FROM THE HEART

I have often thought that the human heart is much like an iceberg, where what we see of one another is only a small amount of who we really are. The fact that most of an iceberg's mass lies underwater is one of its most fascinating characteristics. Typically, about ninety per cent of an iceberg's total mass is hidden beneath the surface, which led to the famous metaphor of something having 'just the tip of the iceberg' visible.

This underwater mass has huge practical implications. During the early days of ocean navigation, it made icebergs particularly dangerous because ships could collide with the massive underwater portions even when trying to steer clear of the visible top. This is what happened with the *Titanic* in 1912 – it's believed the ship struck part of the underwater portion of the iceberg, tearing open its hull.

In much of Christian ministry, as in life generally, people do not see what is really happening below the surface. In fact, we can have similar *Titanic* moments when people sail too close to the hidden issues of our hearts and beneath the surface a collision tears away at our emotional or mental wellbeing.

The Bible uses the heart as a rich metaphor for the inner life of humans, going far beyond just emotions to encompass the whole inner person. In biblical anthropology, the heart represents the core of human personality and the centre of human spiritual and moral life. Unlike modern Western thought, which often separates reason and emotion, the biblical concept of heart integrates thinking, feeling, willing and deciding into one unified centre of human personality.

The heart is the source of thoughts, emotions and decisions (Proverbs 27:19) but is also the place where moral character is formed (Matthew 5:8). The scriptures also recognise that this is the part of the human make-up where spiritual transformation originates (Ezekiel 36:26), the place where God works in his people to bring his light and truth (2 Corinthians 4:6). This understanding of the heart helps explain why biblical transformation is never just about changing behaviour or acquiring knowledge, but about a deep renewal of the whole inner person, starting with the heart. This transformation cannot be possible, though, unless we understand what is at the very core of a healthy heart.

THE GREAT COMMANDMENT

Jesus had a way of simplifying profound truths as the Pharisees sought to trap him in theological complexities.

> *One of them, an expert in the law, tested him with this question: 'Teacher, which is the greatest commandment in the Law?' Jesus replied: '"Love the Lord your God with all your heart and with all your soul and with all your mind." This is the first and greatest commandment. And the second is like it: "Love your neighbour as yourself." All the Law and the Prophets hang on these two commandments.'* (Matthew 22:35-40)

I particularly love the last phrase when Jesus explains that everything that the law contains, or the prophets spoke, is summed up in these two great statements: love God and love people! We must also be careful that we don't lose the simplicity of the life we have been called to. These two requirements of Jesus are still the hallmark for a healthy heart.

Loving God

I have learned that truly loving those you lead becomes almost impossible if you do not truly love the one who leads you. These two corresponding loves are at the heart of what Jesus is saying to Peter after the famous breakfast on the beach with the disciples. In fact, loving Jesus is at the very heart of everything. Life is so difficult to navigate without our hearts being captivated by love for our Saviour.

In my ministry of developing, coaching and mentoring leaders I invariably find that our single greatest challenge is keeping the flames of our affection for God alight. There is so much in the daily life of a leader that will endanger this relationship. We can preach on its importance for those we lead and teach, we can sing songs about our love and affection for God, but only we know how strongly, or not, our love for God burns. I have known that sinking feeling on too many occasions. That moment when I realise that I have become consumed with my role and responsibilities as a leader. I might try to explain that I haven't had time to add fuel to the passion in my heart for God, but my protestations all fall short eventually. Nothing matters more in life than loving Jesus!

This relationship, made possible by what the Son of God did for humanity at the cross, is the centrepiece of life and leadership. It is in my connection with Christ that my heart is formed like his and, as a result, the possibility that my actions will also be more like his. The one who shepherds us loves us in a way that we can never fully understand. Unconditionally, eternally, completely.

If you are just setting out on your journey of Christian leadership then I would counsel you from the bottom of my heart: make him your number-one priority. It's right that you would want to grow in your ability and competence as a shepherd-leader. There is nothing wrong with wanting to be an excellent communicator of God's word. But nothing will shape you as a leader more than knowing his heart for you and allowing him to shape your heart.

Maybe you are like me, a seasoned Christian leader. You have been involved in leading people for decades and look back today with regret that you haven't invested more in being closer to the one who called you. Please don't be overwhelmed by regret. Don't beat yourself up. That ends up being a huge waste of time. Firstly, because God is not beating you up, and secondly, because you waste the energy you can use to make a difference today. What is in yesterday can never be re-lived, but today and tomorrow presents us with the opportunity for something new. Every day affords us a new opportunity to commit afresh to our relationship with God.

You could even pause now, put this book down and allow yourself some moments to turn your attention towards Jesus. Ask the Holy Spirit to focus the lens of your soul so that any distractions around you blend into the background and the person of Jesus becomes clearly seen. Wait in that place and ask him to draw you closer.

Are you back with me now? I almost don't want to move on because I want you to know that moments like that, if you did pause to be with him, are precious and priceless. They are the moments we can never get enough of. They don't have to last for hours, because one brief encounter with Jesus can be totally transforming. Think about how you can make those moments more regular, even when life is chaotic.

As I write these reflections, I am thinking of how I have found the last few months in my little world very chaotic. My thoughts and emotions have been stretched, and whilst I can normally juggle many activities and tasks, I have been so aware of the weight of some of the issues I am caught up in. Yet these are the very moments when I, like you, need to pause and be with him.

Recently, Amanda and I were visiting our son and his family in Norfolk. The weather was glorious, which was great because the early part of the summer here in the UK had been awful (not unusual). Matthew and his family have a wonderful Cavapoo named Sherlock. Though my family never had dogs when I was growing up, I have grown to love Sherlock and love taking him for walks when I can.

That hot summer morning my canine buddy and I were strolling through some nearby fields as I poured my heart out to God about the things that were making me anxious. As my words ended, I clearly heard the voice of the Spirit remind me of a verse of scripture that immediately filled me with genuine serenity. I remembered it from my Sunday school days in the King James Version: 'Thou wilt keep him in perfect peace, whose mind is stayed on thee: because he trusteth in thee' (Isaiah 26:3).

This is what he can do for your heart too. It is in keeping our heart connected to his that the pressures and challenges of life as a shepherd-leader are managed. I suspect that those leaders we know who fell or failed might tell us that this priority slipped down the to-do list. It may be that all kinds of things they were striving for took more of their time and energies than keeping their hearts close to Jesus. Christian leadership has become way more complex than when I set out on my journey in the late 1980s. But that cannot be an excuse for not maintaining the health of my walk with Jesus.

Loving people

Have you ever noticed how open the apostle Paul was about his feelings? He really did wear his heart on his sleeve, as we would say. He is not a heartless disciplinarian but rather he shows a genuine compassion and tender heart for those he felt responsibility for.

To the Thessalonians he says: 'Just as a nursing mother cares for her children, so we cared for you. Because we loved you so much, we were delighted to share with you not only the gospel of God but our lives as well' (1 Thessalonians 2:7-8).

To the very challenging church in Corinth, he says: 'I will very gladly spend for you everything I have and expend myself as well. If I love you more, will you love me less?' (2 Corinthians 12:15).

To one of his favourite churches in Philippi he says: 'I have you in my heart and . . . God can testify how I long for all of you with the affection of Christ Jesus' (Philippians 1:7-8).

These are very affectionate words, particularly in the era of history in which Paul wrote. But this is the heart of shepherd-leadership. Loving people is what we are called to do, even when they are not easy to love. Following the shepherd call means you need to be prepared for your heart to experience joy in wonderful ways but also to know pain in equally significant measure.

Too many leaders insulate themselves by hiding their heart away from people. They retreat into a formalism that means wearing a mask to avoid people knowing them and experiencing an authenticity in relationship. As I sit and type these words, I can think of people I haven't seen for many years who I still feel genuine affection for. Some of them are in heaven now, but I remember the moments when they opened their hearts to me and shared their deepest thoughts and fears.

In some cases, they opened areas of their lives that they had not talked about with others. Many shepherd-leaders carry deeply private stories that have been shared with them. This privilege, though, is rarely offered to a leader who has not modelled an openness of heart to those they are shepherding.

This kind of relationship is the foundation upon which all other aspects of shepherd-leadership is built. This *knowing* is what is described in John 10 when Jesus says, 'I know my sheep and my sheep know me' (John 10:14). But this may not be true in some church settings. It may be that the sheep have no real contact with the shepherd, and the shepherd could walk past one of those they are leading in the supermarket and have no clue who they are.

Shepherds who retreat from the platform to the green room will only ever get to know those who share the Sunday stage with them. In one very large church I visit occasionally, I am always thrilled to see the senior pastor standing at the door after church, chatting to people as they leave and building connections with them. It is possible for people to feel loved, even in larger churches, and it is possible for people to feel remote from their shepherd in small churches. The size of the church is rarely the problem, the heart of the shepherd is.

Like many of my peers in ministry I was taught that people don't really care about what you know, until they know that you really care. Too often we have become consumed with leadership competency at the expense of leadership affection. When Jesus addresses Peter's denial of him in John 21 he doesn't challenge Peter's competence or courage but his affection, first for Christ himself and then for the people the Master wants him to care for: '"Simon son of John, do you love me more than these?" "Yes, Lord," he said, "you know that I love you." Jesus said, "Feed my lambs"' (John 21:15).

Of course, loving people extends beyond the doors of the church family. Shepherd-leaders are not only called to love those who they see as part of their church family, but to lead the church family to love their community, town or city. No-one modelled loving lost people more than Jesus. Having a heart like his, is to love those who don't fit into the religious moulds that Christendom has historically created. Saying you love people in your church gatherings will be tested the moment someone walks through the doors who doesn't fit the mould your church has subconsciously created.

Jesus fell out with the religious leaders of his day because they couldn't understand why he had time for tax collectors, prostitutes, lepers and Gentiles. Jesus loved people, and he loved them the same if they were his followers or if they were his enemies. That is the measurement for loving people and it's a very high bar to clear.

The heart of the shepherd-leader is the place we lead from. Loving and leading people may well be the most emotionally demanding thing that you do with your life. That is why the condition of our hearts is critical to the way we can love and lead people. You may not even realise how much the condition of your heart shapes the way you lead. So, it would be good to examine how much of the way we live our lives is formed in that secret, quiet place we call the heart.

THE CRUCIBLE WHERE OUR LIVES ARE FORMED

Some shepherd-leaders can make the mistake of focusing too much on the external and visible activities of ministry and not on the internal and invisible condition of our lives. We are regularly reminded of the need to guard our heart (Proverbs 4:23) and have found that this is the work that requires most of us. Tom Nelson explains the reality that most shepherd-leaders find when he says: 'If we are brutally honest, pursuing greater wholeness in our lives is often where we expend our greatest energies. Whether it's a fallen pastoral colleague or a fallen tree, this may be a wake-up call that our own soul is the first work of leadership.'[19]

As leaders, many of us have forgotten how vulnerable our hearts are. God speaks to Jeremiah to remind him that the heart is deceitful above all things (Jeremiah 17:9). All our decisions and choices in life begin here, in the melting pot of our thoughts and emotions. It's a very tender place, unseen by even those closest to us.

The beauty and challenge of tenderness

Tenderness is at the heart of shepherd-leadership. A tender heart is a heart that cares and is touched by the needs and pains of those we love and lead. Yet this very tenderness means we can be damaged, as we will see in a later chapter when we explore the wounds that shepherd-leaders can easily experience as they seek to love and serve people.

I have found shepherd-leadership has stretched the capacity of my heart in so many ways. Sometimes it's the agony of being unable to change a situation for someone who is in great need, but on other occasions it has been dealing with the anxieties that I feel, the inadequacies that often make many of us, as shepherd-leaders, feel incapable of the task given to us by the Lord himself.

Yet it seems it was this tender place that attracted God to David, the young shepherd, who he chose to become the king of his people Israel. We know very little of David's early years until we meet him on the occasion that Samuel is sent by God to anoint the next king of Israel from among Jesse's sons. Among all the qualities that Samuel considered most appropriate for the next king of Israel, God had only one attribute that mattered to him: 'People look at the outward appearance, but the Lord looks at the heart' (1 Samuel 16:7).

David could not be considered a man, or leader, who was faultless. His heart for God is clear but his weakness and sinfulness is also evident. He failed to control his emotions and desires when he should have gone back to his bed after seeing Bathsheba bathing and afforded her the dignity of some privacy. He didn't, and what followed not only led to adultery but murder.

How could David be considered a man 'after God's own heart' (1 Samuel 13:14)? It may well be that the answer to this probing question is found in David's genuine repentance when challenged by the prophet Nathan. This is where his famous prayer in Psalm 51 originates: 'Create in me a pure heart, O God...' A heart that doesn't hide in iniquity has the greatest chance of healing and restoration.

Moments of grace and healing

Throughout my years serving as a local church pastor, I never claimed to be faultless. In fact, those I led will tell you that I regularly described myself as fallible and sometimes even feeling weak. People have maybe viewed me as far more confident than I know myself to be. Much of that comes from my extrovert personality, yet behind the scenes of my public ministry you will find a man who has often wept before the Lord because of my own sense of weakness and feelings of inadequacy.

I remember one Sunday morning when I got up quite early, as was the norm, to get ready for the day's services which started at 9.00am. I genuinely can't remember why I woke up with such deep feelings of guilt and condemnation, but I vividly remember being overwhelmed as I lay on the lounge floor, weeping before the Lord whilst my family all slept upstairs. I was wishing that I didn't have to lead three services that Sunday as if I were pretending to be something I thought I was not.

I remember saying to the Lord that here I was again, asking him for his grace to somehow try to find feelings of adequacy that could equip me to stand before the people I served. In a moment of real clarity, I heard the Holy Spirit whisper into my soul as he said to me, 'Don't say "again" again.' Instantly, my mind was filled with the words from Psalm 103, which reminded me that 'as far as the east is from the west, so far has he removed our transgressions from us' (Psalm 103:12).

It meant so much to me that when I went to church that morning, I put to one side the well-crafted message that had taken much of Friday to prepare and, with courage and honesty, opened my Bible at Psalm 103. I stood beside the communion table and spoke vulnerably about my experience that morning with the church family. I reminded them that the communion that we were about to share was a constant reminder that we never stand in our own righteousness, but in the righteousness given to us in Christ.

God visited us in a special way that morning and I've never preached that message again because it was for that moment. But it remained with me as a constant reminder that God promises to meet me in my weakness. I suppose it also taught me the value of keeping my heart tender before God, not feeling I needed to hide that from those I was leading. Reminding them that I, too, failed the Lord and daily need his grace.

Why is it that the very characteristic that seemed to attract God to the young David is not readily celebrated today among leaders? Why is it that we talk about the importance of a tender heart but are keen to hide our vulnerabilities from those we lead?

Maintaining the garden of our hearts

The heart is the place we cannot hide from God. It is the place he forms who we are. The place where the great qualities of shepherd-leadership like compassion, integrity, authenticity, humility and passion are stirred and moulded. When we neglect the condition of our hearts, we find that it does not make itself well. When describing the emotional and spiritual deficits of what an unhealthy heart looks like, Peter Scazzero says: 'Unhealthy leaders lack awareness of their feelings, their weaknesses and limits, how the past impacts the present, and how others experience them.'[20]

As a very reluctant gardener I am aware that if I leave our garden, the weeds will grow and they will suffocate the good plants we have. However much I may go and weed the garden, they will come back. The lesson I learn from this is that maintaining my heart is a constant exercise of surrender to the Lord and asking him to show me where I need his forgiveness or healing inside me. In another famous prayer, David asks the Lord to look at how his heart is doing: 'Search me, God, and know my heart; test me and know my anxious thoughts. See if there is any offensive way in me, and lead me in the way everlasting' (Psalm 139:23-24).

Maybe this is something you realise you have neglected. Please don't believe the lie that your heart is beyond repair. It never is. As we will see in a later chapter, even the wounds we experience can be healed and empower our shepherd-leadership. What is critically important is that you are a shepherd-leader who takes the necessary time to reflect on the condition of your heart. I've discovered that those leaders I mix with who practise honest self-reflection, are usually healthier than the ones I know who seem to refuse to acknowledge any kind of unhealthy habits, attitudes or perspectives.

7
THE TITLE OR THE TOWEL

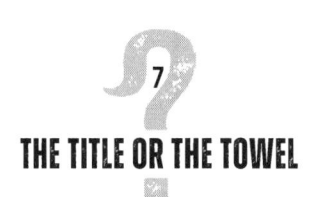

A few years ago, I was scrolling through Facebook when I saw a post from one of the young Bible college graduates who had recently been interviewed for ministry in the Elim movement. His passion and enthusiasm were obvious, and his vision for what was next in his ministry was clear to all who caught a few minutes with him. Yet when I saw his post, it became instantly apparent to me that he had fallen into the trap that so many of us do when we get that acceptance into a more formal recognition of ministry. He wrote: *'You can call me Pastor now.'* I didn't want to dampen his joy in being accepted into the first stages of his training for ministry but couldn't resist replying: *'I'll do that when I see some sheep following you.'*

I am thankful that the denomination I have served for nearly four decades isn't overly concerned with titles, because I do know of some other streams of the church where this seems hugely important. In fact, I remember being asked the question *'Should we call you pastor?'* by one lovely lady when I moved to Christian Life Centre in 1994. She was thankfully humoured by my reply: *'I'm very happy for you to call me Stuart, because that's what my mum named me.'*

We have made so much of titles in the Christian church. Words that are used by Paul in his letters to churches in the first century to describe the gifts that Christ has gifted to his church are still used as badges of honour by some who seem to have missed the point. Whilst we almost always use the prefix *apostle* to identify Paul, he was keen to distance himself from such titles. He didn't shy away from the fact that he had been called to be an apostle in the introduction to a number of his letters, but at the same time he would refer to himself as the 'least of the apostles' (1 Corinthians 15:9) whilst at the same time being confident in his calling, even if others didn't consider him to be equal to the 'super apostles' (2 Corinthians 11:5). It seems that even in the early church there was a pecking order already established in the minds of some that Paul wanted to disassociate himself from.

I confess that in the early years of my ministry it felt good to be recognised for the call of God on my life, and with it to feel that people respected the responsibilities that such a calling gave me. When people called me pastor it meant something. But quite quickly I realised that titles alone can never give you the assurance that can only come from the affirmation God himself speaks over us, whether we serve in public Christian ministry or not. I cringe sometimes when I hear some leaders insist that their position and authority be recognised by using one or more titles that frankly mean nothing if we are not living and leading in the pattern of the Good Shepherd. Such hierarchical expectations say much more about the insecurity of a leader than they do about their ability or capacity.

WHEN LEADERSHIP BECOMES SELF-SERVING

Most Christian leaders do not set out to be accused of misusing the influence that comes with the roles they occupy, but there are some who just want to be noticed, recognised and heard. This need to be recognised can sometimes sadly lead to an unhealthy emphasis on the leader alone, the title they carry, or a set of expectations they have that can prove damaging if unchecked.

Self-centred leadership is very dangerous, but not unusual in all walks of life. The reason for this is that word *self*. It is at the root of insecurity and is the cause of many a mistake that can be made in the honourable pursuit of leadership. There again is another word we have got wrong in the church too often, *honour*. It has become a notion that entitles some to deference, reward and the avoidance of healthy scrutiny. Tony Morgan, the founder of the Unstuck Group, has written:

> *Some churches are trying to create a culture where all the 'underlings' are supposed to honour their senior pastor by serving his every need, by guarding him from the congregation and by always saying 'yes sir' to every request among other things. Being armour-bearers to each other is one thing – when it creeps into making the pastor the 'king,' it's a completely different deal.[21]*

Of course, he refers to the *culture of honour* that has become an important idea in some parts of the church. And whilst there is obviously an encouragement in scripture for honouring those who 'direct the affairs of the church well . . . especially those whose work is preaching and teaching' (1 Timothy 5:17), this is not a mandate for building higher podiums and platforms (metaphorically speaking) for some leaders. Genuinely respecting those who lead us is a healthy thing and something that the scriptures encourage. But it also comes with a health warning for us in our generation. Tim Keller summarises this balance very well, 'Honouring leadership is not about blind obedience, but about recognising the God-given responsibility and burden that leaders carry. It's a way of partnering in the mission of the church.'[22]

The tension between honour and humility in leadership isn't new to our generation. In fact, this struggle was present even among Jesus' closest followers. The desire for recognition and position – that subtle pull towards elevating ourselves above others – has been challenging God's people since the earliest days of the church. We see this clearly illustrated in one of the most revealing moments in the gospels, when the mother of James and John approached Jesus with a bold request.

THE ROOT OF ENTITLEMENT

It's fascinating that the mother of Jesus' disciples, James and John, felt she could make a request of Jesus that her boys could occupy the seats of honour on the right and left of Jesus in the kingdom to come (Matthew 20:21). I remember as a teenager seeing the wonderful musical *The Witness* by Jimmy and Carol Owens. There was one very funny song called 'My Boys', that portrayed this scene in the gospels. It was a mum who thought her boys were just the best and deserved to be seated beside the King of kings in the eternal kingdom. She meant well, and her love for her sons was admirable, but Jesus had to quickly remind her, and the disciples, that high position is not what leads to greatness.

Have you ever visited a church or a conference that has seats of honour? Or have you observed when the preacher can't even carry their own Bible to the pulpit or needs bodyguards to protect them from the people who they want to be excited by every word that drips from their mouth? Have we gone wrong somewhere? What should honouring our leaders really look like?

I was invited for a few years to speak at a small conference in a hotel in central Birmingham. It was run by a small church and had little more than a hundred and twenty people present. As I arrived, I was assigned an enthusiastic young man who was keen to carry my Bible and escort me to a special seat at the front. I was happy for him to guide me to a seat but couldn't quite understand why he felt I may be too weak to carry my pretty small Bible. Of course, he was simply carrying out what he had been told to do, all in the name of honouring the 'man of God'. I watched as other so-called men and women of God arrived and strutted to their special seats with their assigned courier carrying their Bible with proper respect.

However much I'm told these are cultural expectations or simply ways to honour men and women of God, I still struggle to reconcile such patterns of behaviour with the servant example of Jesus. The problem of entitlement exists in all denominations and streams of the church. It may not always be visible in someone's actions, but it can exist in their attitudes. The greater the popularity a leader receives, the greater the challenge to 'guard your heart' (Proverbs 4:23). We have seen the tragedy of well-known leaders exposed for a variety of mistakes they have made. But have we considered whether the genesis of these problems was a sense of entitlement?

'I deserve to be treated well.'

'I've worked hard to get where I am.'

'I made sacrifices you didn't see and so have earned this level of respect.'

Yet these are not just the thoughts of some of those high-profile leaders whose reputations are now tarnished, they are a problem for all of us in leadership. They are the thoughts we battle with at 3.00am after a difficult elders' meeting, or as we deal with the torment of criticism or disagreement. As Dr Noe Garcia has observed, 'Faithful pastoring mixed with what feels like unfaithful responses from church members can leave you destructively bitter. When the seed of bitterness is planted the fruit of entitlement is produced.'[23]

All this may seem negative and critical, particularly of some of those leaders whose gifts and success have made them well known. My aim is not to caricature popular leaders in the church, but sadly I don't think I'm the only one who feels that the effects of the excesses we have heard about in some Christian leaders has been to paint all Christian leaders with a brush that most don't deserve to be tarnished with.

I fear that in some circles the entitlement that leaders have embraced, and often excused, may be irreversible. But if it is reversible, it will be by a generation of leaders who reject such selfish pursuits in favour of the vicarious servant spirit that we see in the greatest example of leadership to grace this planet.

JESUS, THE SERVANT LEADER

Nowhere do we find a greater example of servant leadership than in Jesus himself. The regular arguments among the disciples about who was the greatest must have been very tiring, and even frustrating for Jesus. But as usual he had a way of teaching them something they would never forget. Something that was shocking and counter-cultural. He washed their feet.

> *The evening meal was in progress, and the devil had already prompted Judas, the son of Simon Iscariot, to betray Jesus. Jesus knew that the Father had put all things under his power, and that he had come from God and was returning to God; so, he got up from the meal, took off his outer clothing, and wrapped a towel around his waist. After that, he poured water into a basin and began to wash his disciples' feet, drying them with the towel that was wrapped around him.* (John 13:2-5)

In the days in which Jesus lived on earth, foot-washing was a normal practice that took place before a meal. The disciples' view of Jesus as a rabbi and their gradual acceptance of his divine identity made this a radical display of humility. The disciples wouldn't have even thought to wash each other's feet, let alone the feet of someone with lower status than themselves. Jesus chose the towel not the title. He demonstrates to his disciples that nothing is beneath those who have placed themselves beneath God's authority. Philip Greenslade describes John 13 as spelling out for us the style of leadership on which our own is to be based.[24] Here we see that Jesus is so secure in who he is that he is free to serve.

William Barclay has expressed the tensions of this example of Jesus so well, when he says:

> *This ought to make us think. So often, even in churches, trouble arises because someone does not get his place.*

> *So often even ecclesiastical dignitaries are offended because they did not receive the precedence to which their office entitled them.*[25]

Let's be candid: it is happening all the time in churches. Little signs of vanishing humility. Clearly, gratitude can wear thin when we feel somehow slighted by others, however unintentional. A colleague gets the move to a bigger church you feel you deserved, so you won't speak to them again. One of the vocalists isn't asked to sing the lead in the new song so leaves the worship team in protest. Your elders forget the anniversary weekend of your arrival to lead the church five years ago, so you cancel the regular elders' meeting in a sulk because you feel dishonoured.

This isn't the kind of leadership attitude that Jesus displayed on this occasion when he knelt in front of his disciples with their dirty feet in his hands. I can only imagine that none of them ever forgot this moment. Towel moments are rarely forgotten by those who receive them.

THE PARADOX OF SERVICE

When I was growing up there were only three TV channels in the UK, and so certain shows achieved huge popularity among the British public. One of those was *Upstairs, Downstairs*. In this widely loved TV production, the lives and fortunes of the Bellamy family and their below-stairs servant staff at 165 Eaton Place, play out against the social, political and historical backdrop of Edwardian London from 1903 to 1930. Richard Bellamy MP and his actress wife Gail, along with their three children, are served daily by those who live and work in the basement of their grand London townhouse. The butler, Frank Hudson, and cook, Mrs Bridges, are helped by maids who care for every need of the Bellamy family. The masters upstairs control the fortunes of the servants downstairs.

My fascination with this show was influenced by my gran, who would tell stories of when she, as a young teenage girl, worked in service for a wealthy family. We would often talk about how Gran learned to starch all the bedsheets in those years when she worked as a maid with the downstairs servants. For a more recent generation *Downton Abbey* has relived this period of British history, when wealth, status and class distinctions placed you in a life of either grand privilege or working-class servitude. As Rick Warren explains, 'The world defines greatness in terms of power, possessions, prestige, and position. If you can demand service from others, you've arrived.'[26] But in the kingdom of God, service is the way to greatness. The only way up is down.

Service is something to be celebrated

Maybe as a result we have developed a view of serving that diminishes what Jesus taught and modelled himself. The incident we looked at earlier when the mother of James and John asked for seats of honour for *her boys*, leads to some remarkable words from Jesus.

> *You know that the rulers of the Gentiles lord it over them, and their high officials exercise authority over them. Not so with you. Instead, whoever wants to become great among you must be your servant, and whoever wants to be first must be your slave – just as the Son of Man did not come to be served, but to serve, and to give his life as a ransom for many.*
> (Matthew 20:25-28)

Servanthood seems to be something Jesus celebrated. And whatever Jesus celebrated must be of enormous value. It's a dangerous attitude to have that leadership is greater than servanthood. As Eugene H. Peterson said, 'Do you want to stand out? Then step down. Be a servant. If you puff yourself up, you'll get the wind knocked out of you. But if you're content to simply be yourself, your life will count for plenty' (Matthew 23:11-12 *The Message*).

Service is the greatest thing we do

I believe it's time to turn the church upside down. We cannot allow there to be an upstairs of leadership and downstairs of servanthood. Jesus is clear that service is the greatest thing that we can do. It's not a question of whether you are too big to serve but whether you are big enough to serve. One of my good friends, and my Elim Regional Leader for many years, Gordon Neale, would tell us as pastors to do one thing every day to remind ourselves that we are servants. Never has that advice been more important. Too often acts of service are seen as a chore, something that ought to be done. Yet giving ourselves in service to God and people is surely the highest use of our time and talents. The apostle Paul certainly considered that everything he did for others was inspired by his desire to serve God, 'Serve wholeheartedly, as if you were serving the Lord, not people' (Ephesians 6:7).

Service is its own reward

Sadly, we live at a time when some people expect a reward for everything they do. I am grateful for the Lord reminding me recently that service is its own reward. The reward for the energy we expend in loving people is that *we* get to do it. The call on our lives as shepherd-leaders means that people come to us, trust us, listen to us, pray for us and care for us.

What a reward! What a blessing it is to be one of those who God has chosen to serve his people and his world. Of course it isn't easy, serving rarely is. But getting up every morning to do the things that Jesus did has to be the greatest inspiration for how we live. This inverted understanding of reward – where the act of service itself becomes the blessing – perfectly reflects the revolutionary nature of Jesus' kingdom values.

The kingdom of God seems to invert almost all the stories of greatness that we grew up learning. The strong, intelligent, charismatic and popular leader stands at the front of the queue, with everyone else lined up behind them. But how Jesus represents greatness is very different in the King's new order. This is greatness as Jesus modelled it:

> *Who, being in very nature God, did not consider equality with God something to be used to his own advantage; rather, he made himself nothing by taking the very nature of a servant, being made in human likeness. And being found in appearance as a man, he humbled himself by becoming obedient to death – even death on a cross!* (Philippians 2:6-8)

This profound description of Jesus's divine humility wasn't just theological poetry – it was lived out in vivid, practical ways throughout his ministry. Nowhere do we find a greater example of servant leadership than in Jesus himself.

CHOOSING THE TOWEL

In the quiet moments before a Sunday service, when the building stands empty and expectant, every shepherd-leader faces a choice. It's the choice that challenged Jesus' disciples when they argued about greatness, the choice that pastors face when scrolling through social media. Will we hide behind a title, or will we pick up the towel?

The allure of recognition runs deep in church culture. We've witnessed the subtle shift from servant to celebrity, from shepherd to CEO. Yet Jesus' example stands in stark contrast to our cultural instincts. The one who held all authority chose to take off some clothing, wrap a towel around his waist and kneel before his disciples. He didn't just teach servant leadership; he embodied it.

This isn't about refusing to be called 'Pastor' or rejecting all forms of organisational structure. Rather, it's about understanding that true authority flows from authentic service, not from titles or positions. When Jesus washed his disciples' feet, he didn't diminish his authority –

he demonstrated its proper use. He showed us that greatness in God's kingdom looks remarkably different from greatness in our world.

The problem isn't in the positions we hold, but in how we hold them. Do we grasp our titles like badges of honour, or do we wear them lightly, seeing them as opportunities to serve more effectively? Do we use our authority to create distance between ourselves and others, or do we use it to draw alongside people in their moments of need? The towel Jesus used wasn't just a prop for a lesson; it was a symbol of a revolutionary leadership style that would turn the world's hierarchy upside down.

Today's church needs leaders who aren't afraid to choose the towel – who find their security not in titles but in their identity as servants of Christ. This means creating cultures where service is celebrated above status, where the measure of leadership is not in how many people serve us but in how many people we serve. Let's be honest: choosing the towel isn't glamorous. It might mean staying after church to stack chairs when everyone else has gone home. It might mean cleaning up a mess you didn't make or serving in ways that will never be noticed or celebrated. It might mean making coffee for your team or giving someone else the credit that others aim at you. But these moments – these towel moments – are where true leadership is formed and where lasting impact is made.

So, let's look for those towel moments. Let's celebrate them when we see them in others. Let's create cultures in our churches where the towel is more honoured than the title. Because in the end, it won't be the positions we held or the titles we carried that define our legacy – it will be the lives we touched through humble, faithful service. Just as Jesus showed us, true greatness isn't found in rising above others, but in kneeling before them with a towel in hand and love in our hearts.

8
THE WEIGHT OF LEADERSHIP

Leadership isn't just about carrying responsibility. It is about carrying it whilst so many other things stand in opposition to you as a leader. It is carrying it when you are tired as well as when you are energised. Carrying it when everyone is cheering for you, as much as when they are shouting against you.

I have believed for a long time that only those who serve as shepherd-leaders really understand what it feels like to carry this divinely given responsibility. Pastor and blogger Scott Slayton says:

> *Every serious pastor labours under a heavy weight. This is not belly aching or an embellishment, but rather this is the reality of being a pastor. The work is serious, and the work has eternal ramifications. We have the burden of walking with people through the most difficult times of their lives, the pain of sleepless nights because of anxiety over the church, the task of preaching God's word on a weekly basis, and the joy of seeing God use it all for his glory.*[27]

For twenty-two years I led a local church in Birmingham, which was a deeply fulfilling season of my life. During those years I grew immensely as a person and a leader as Amanda and I were surrounded by people who cared for us and supported us in so many ways. When I first arrived at the church I was only twenty-eight years old and still learning what it meant to carry the responsibility for a group of people who deeply longed for God. I had spent the previous four years leading a church in High Wycombe, which though small was extremely loving and encouraging.

I could not have foreseen how the sense of responsibility would grow exponentially in this new setting. Along with it would come a weight, that I felt on so many occasions, for the circumstances in people's lives, the important decisions we needed to make as leaders, and even the expectation that I could provide answers to hugely challenging situations. I carried all that, and more, for over two decades without always realising the effect it was having on me.

A few months after leaving that church, which was wrenching us away from people and a place we loved deeply, I had something of an epiphany. Two realisations dawned on me one day as I reflected with the Lord the sense of loss I was feeling. The first was the loss of relationships. I realised that some friends were church friends, and when we were no longer part of the life of that church, our friendships grew increasingly distant. It should not be a surprise that our relationships drifted because we were not in community together anymore and seeking to serve the mission of Jesus together. It was not an easy recognition because I thrive as part of social settings. But it was an honest appraisal of how our life had changed.

The second realisation was more positive, but it also revealed to me something very deeply significant about the life of someone who leads a local church. I remember vividly feeling 'look what responsibility I'm not carrying'. It was that dawning realisation that for so many years I had not noticed the weight of responsibility and expectation that sat on my life. I suppose I had learned to carry it like someone does a rucksack, when over a lengthy journey either you or others have increasingly added weight to what you carry, even if those weights formed only small measures, they all mounted up to an overwhelming sense of responsibility.

Those weights come in lots of different forms. Some, in and of themselves, are positive things. But some are negative and placed upon us by others. Many leaders find these expectations difficult to carry and refusing to do so can be dependent upon the circumstances in which they lead.

Reflecting on the uniqueness of the shepherd-leader role, Scott Slayton says:

> *In one sense, pastors have a difficult job just like everyone else in the world. We all work in a world marred by sin and know the experience of work being hard, uncomfortable, and unenjoyable. At the same time, because of the unique calling involved in leading a church, proclaiming God's word, and caring for souls, the pastoral ministry carries a gravity that is difficult to explain.[28]*

I suppose when I had the realisation of carrying less weight, I was acknowledging that the Sunday we said farewell to a church we loved I had removed that rucksack of responsibility from my emotional and spiritual shoulders and left it behind. As I look back from the role I find myself in today, I realise that period was short lived. I was forging a new role in Elim and those early months presented very few expectations other than the opportunity to create something that would bring value to our movement. That certainly is not the case today. In fact, as I write I am at the beginning of a sabbatical that is allowing me time to reflect once more on the rucksack of responsibilities that I now carry. They are quite different from my role as a shepherd in the local church, but nevertheless they feel weighty at times, particularly in recent months, and have weighed very heavily upon my soul.

As I reflect on my own journey of carrying and eventually recognising these leadership weights, I've come to understand that my experience echoes through the centuries of spiritual leadership. The burdens I felt in Birmingham and now feel in a different way in my current role, are not unique to our modern context or to my situation. They are part of a profound pattern woven into the very fabric of shepherd-leadership throughout biblical and church history. When we examine the testimonies of those who have gone before us, we find that the weight of spiritual responsibility has always been a defining aspect of leading God's people.

THE WEIGHT WE CARRY

Many of you reading this will easily associate with those feelings of burden that ministry responsibilities bring to us. We are not alone. This is not new in the history of God calling men and women to serve him. The saints of old lived in vastly different circumstances from those that we live in today, but they felt the weight of the responsibility for the souls of those who they led very deeply.

Moses felt that weight as he led Israel through the tough terrain of the wilderness, and the effects it was having on their morale.

> *Why have you brought this trouble on your servant? What have I done to displease you that you put the burden of all these people on me? Did I conceive all these people? Did I give them birth? Why do you tell me to carry them in my arms, as a nurse carries an infant, to the land you promised on oath to their ancestors? Where can I get meat for all these people? They keep wailing to me, 'Give us meat to eat!' I cannot carry all these people by myself; the burden is too heavy for me.* (Numbers 11:11-14)

Paul felt that weight as he wrote to the churches that were springing up in the early gospel movement across the world, whilst coping with the mistreatment and privations he was experiencing as he sought to spread the gospel.

> *I have laboured and toiled and have often gone without sleep; I have known hunger and thirst and have often gone without food; I have been cold and naked. Besides everything else, I face daily the pressure of my concern for all the churches.* (2 Corinthians 11:27-28)

Jesus felt the weight of cosmic expectation as he paused in the garden of Gethsemane before the most challenging moments of his time on this planet, when he would carry the weight and burden of not just our sin but the sin of all humankind, past, present and future, to the cross. He asks the Father if there is anyway this could be taken from him, and yet he still declared, 'Not my will, but yours be done' (Luke 22:42).

These words of Jesus are the most helpful perspective we can find. We know that the responsibilities we carry as shepherd-leaders are weighty, but they just do not compare with all that Jesus carried. They are, however, real, and at times hugely demanding. Carey Nieuwhof describes this in one of his regular blogs: 'The weight of leadership is the sense of responsibility you carry that goes with your job. The problem is it never turns off easily. It follows you home. It accompanies you to bed. It travels with you on vacation.'[29] These weights come in so many different forms and the ones I highlight here are only illustrative of many of the things that shepherd-leadership might ask of us.

Criticism

This ever-increasing challenge faces leaders all the time. Sometimes people's complaints are justifiable, but the way they express them is not. On occasions the comments might be totally unjustified and therefore even harder to carry. It is, nevertheless, one of the weightiest parts of leadership as it can strike at the self-esteem of a leader who may be trying their very best. Criticism itself is not always a bad thing; in fact, there is usually some truth in most criticism. The weightier part of this is often the way someone expresses themselves and when their motivation is to damage the leader it can become an unbearable burden in our souls.

Conflict

Church life can be a messy and distressing environment. I know we should expect better of each other but that doesn't change the fact that we don't do conflict well in church most of the time. Whilst we all serve the Prince of Peace, many shepherds and their flocks end up in bitter squabbles or, worse, distressing battles. Hugh Halverstadt has summarised this frustrating ambiguity well:

> *Christians fight, they also fight dirty. Issues get personalized. Gossip and hearsay fog up reason and common sense. Enemy-making wounds shred long-standing friendships. It is no wonder that so many thoughtful Christians avoid church conflicts like the plagues of Egypt.*[30]

I have seen what such conflicts can do to shepherd-leaders and sheep alike. It is the saddest of all representations of the church to the world and yet we (because all of us need to take responsibility) never seem to learn. The weight of such conflicts will usually leave a lifelong scar on a leader.

Expectation

It can feel a very heavy thing to try to live up to what others expect of us. We are aware that some of those expectations are either misplaced or unrealistic. This is where those in church leadership will understand the pressures of various people or groups in their congregation who have their own preferences, and even feelings of entitlement, because of their longevity in the church or the level of their financial giving.

Alongside these kinds of expectations is the challenge to produce each week. I accept that's maybe not the best way to describe the weekly duty to teach, preach and inspire. But for many shepherd-leaders it is, nonetheless, how they can sometimes feel. Scott Slayton recognises this challenge:

> *The weekly grind of preaching can be mentally, emotionally, and spiritually exhausting if you are taking it seriously. Every week, we wrestle with a passage of Scripture, seeking to understand what it means and how it should change the*

lives of the people who hear it. We labour over the Bible, commentaries, word studies, and points of application. We plead with God to take what we will say and use it for his glory. Then we preach with all our heart and get up on Monday morning to start preparing to do it again.[31]

Integrity

It is a huge challenge when we become aware that the thing that influences people more than our words is our actions. We live on a much higher platform than the one we preach from. How we live is seen as descriptive of what we believe. Preaching one thing and living another is not compatible with shepherd-leadership. People will forget our words far more quickly than they will forget our actions, particularly the negative or damaging ones. As shepherd-leaders we realise that the decisions we make daily affect more people than just ourselves and our family.

Franklin Graham wrote a book collating some of the wisdom of his father, the late Dr Billy Graham. He documents Billy Graham's thoughts on a wide range of topics. Concerning integrity he records his father saying: 'Integrity is the glue that holds our way of life together. We must constantly strive to keep our integrity intact. When wealth is lost, nothing is lost; when health is lost, something is lost; when character is lost, all is lost.'[32]

We know this is true and that is the reason why living in such a way feels such a weighty exercise. Every leader knows that feeling of shame when personal sin, so often hidden from everyone else but God, weighs heavily on our soul. When the enemy's taunts us about our failure and cripples our confidence, we must find our way back to the Saviour and his cleansing.

Disappointment

No leader can avoid disappointment. Shepherd-leaders have certainly experienced how ministry and leadership can be a bruising as well as a joyful life. There are a thousand and one ways that disappointment weighs upon the hearts and minds of those called to serve God. Aspirations that didn't pan out, people who let us down, mistakes we wish we hadn't made, and so many more that I'm sure you could add in the margin here. A lesson I've learned, even in the past year or so, is that disappointment is a reality, but bitterness is a choice. If we cannot avoid the weight of disappointment, maybe we should spend our energy on not allowing it to shape how we live and lead in the future.

As I said earlier, I am certain that you could add many things to the list of things that weigh heavily on those who lead, so maybe it would be good to turn our attention to how we respond to these and finally how what we carry can also strengthen us in the long term.

HOW TO CARRY THE WEIGHT OF LEADERSHIP WELL?

Before answering that question there is something critically important for us to understand. Jesus didn't shy away from telling his followers that there is a burden to carry for those who give themselves to walk in his ways.

However, he did provide a clear distinction between the 'yoke' he gives us from the yoke that others would place on us. I particularly like Eugene H. Peterson's portrayal of Jesus' word in *The Message* version.

> *Are you tired? Worn out? Burned out on religion? Come to me. Get away with me and you'll recover your life. I'll show you how to take a real rest. Walk with me and work with me – watch how I do it. Learn the unforced rhythms of grace. I won't lay anything heavy or ill-fitting on you. Keep company with me and you'll learn to live freely and lightly.* (Matthew 11:28-30)

God's call to shepherd-leadership will mean carrying a weight of responsibility. Ultimately this responsibility is to him, the one who called us. The call of God is not *ill-fitting* to those who are truly called. But Jesus clearly does say that there is something to carry. The secret is that we do not carry it alone. The very idea of a yoke is that it connects two oxen to each other in the hard work of ploughing a field.

The critical question becomes how do we find ways to alleviate ourselves from the weights that we are not designed to carry and, at the same time, how do we find the resources and help on those occasions when we struggle to manage the weights of leadership that are part and parcel of the call of God on our lives?

Be honest with yourself

Carrying any weight you were not designed to carry is debilitating and wearying, but it is made worse if you don't recognise them at all. Too often leaders have blind spots, a lack of self-awareness, to the effects of carrying too much. Even if others who love us express their concerns, unless we see it ourselves, we are often trapped in a place of deceit. Such a place is dark and dangerous for any shepherd-leader and one can rarely climb out on their own. It was a cave like this that God called Elijah out of to face up to what he could not see himself. There, at the mouth of that cave, God teaches him to hear the whisper of his voice, even when wind, earthquake and fire had too much of Elijah's attention (1 Kings 19).

Discern and describe the weights you carry

Measure the weight of what you are carrying and be real if it is affecting you emotionally. If you don't you may pay a very high price in your marriage, family, friendships and your ministry. It always helps to make space to look at your life and leadership through the lens of healthy scrutiny. So often the varied leadership responsibilities we carry can be compounded by personal and family matters that those we lead know nothing about. I know how much this played a part in my own stress during a particularly difficult period of my life. I was trying to hide the pain of what I was experiencing but it ultimately bled into my day-to-day responsibilities, and I struggled to carry it all.

Build your carrying capacity

Having acknowledged that shepherd-leaders need to beware of carrying too much, we should also acknowledge that we are called to serve the purposes of God and grow in our capacity and calling. It will help if you can welcome the weight of your calling as a transforming experience that God himself has initiated. The weight of leadership will do one of two things to you: it will either crush you or it could strengthen your life for greater use by God.

It takes roughly 725,000 pounds of pressure per square inch, and temperatures over 2,200 degrees Fahrenheit, to create a diamond. In other words, a fully loaded Boeing 747 and a blast furnace! So often we look at a diamond and are mesmerised by its beauty and perfection, but we forget the hostile conditions that created the gem.

What do people see when they look into your eyes? Do they see someone whose joy and love for God has been crushed out of them by the pressures of ministry? Or are they inspired by the love, compassion and satisfaction that has been formed through the weight and heat of serving God?

Those who know me might read my thoughts here with a wry smile, as I am certainly no body builder. I won't be found in the gym pumping iron and resembling the latest muscular Adonis to inspire such pursuits. But like most of us, I understand the dynamics of how to build the capacity to carry heavy weights. I've watched those strongman competitions on TV where some muscular man-mountain lifts weight that should really be borne by a forklift truck. I know they acquired that strength over many years of building their muscles. They trained and progressively lifted increasing weights to condition their body to achieve such extraordinary exploits. I'm sure they knew what diet they needed to fuel their physical frame, and they also appreciated the benefits of rest to save their strength for the occasions they needed it most.

Those are the very same principles I believe apply in responsible shepherd-leadership. Those people that you marvel at who seem to effortlessly make huge decisions, and balance enormous responsibilities have also been trained over many years by learning to carry smaller and lesser weights well. Mature and godly spiritual leadership begins in the private place, where the Spirit's tuition of our soul builds muscles of humility, faith, patience, grace, endurance and trust. It is then developed in serving God in sometimes the smallest of opportunities presented to us and progressively believing he can use us to help people in situations we might have previously run from.

In the parable of the talents, the master commends the servants who increased what he had given them with these words: 'Well done, good and faithful servant! You have been faithful with a few things; I will put you in charge of many things' (Matthew 25:21, 23).

The strange thing about building muscle physically is that it requires resistance. The heavier the weight, the greater resistance it creates. I know if I were to want to significantly build my muscles I would need to start with a smaller weight and gradually build my capacity to lift something much heavier. If you are a younger leader, you need to be encouraged that as you gradually increase the leadership weight you may carry you will find your capacity to carry more grows too. In my own journey it was often imperceptible to me. It was others who perceived my increasing capacity as a leader. Others who believed that I could serve God in ways that carried greater influence and responsibility.

Ensure you are not trapped in isolation

The long walk of leadership is often a lonely one. We often talk about the dangers of the sheep that lives on the fringes of the flock, but what about the shepherd who is isolated from their fellow shepherds and, most of all, from the Good Shepherd himself? Brad Lomenick makes a sobering observation in his excellent book *H3 Leadership*: 'Every leader runs the risk of quarantining himself or herself in an ivory tower. Evaluate your own level of isolation by surveying the number and quality of relational connections in your life. Lone Ranger leaders are destined for trouble.'[33]

As leaders, we need to guard against any looming temptation to prefer seclusion. We must refuse to believe isolation is an unavoidable ingredient of our leadership role. This is a lie. We walk in truth when we choose to make intentional connections with our friends, coaches, mentors and leaders. Having positive affirming friendships must be seen as critical to any sphere of healthy leadership and vital to managing the stresses and strains of the life we are called to.

Find leaders who can coach and support you

I remember well the moment during a coaching course I took when I realised that as a fifty-year-old leader I needed someone to coach me too. It was something I hadn't really thought of before. I asked the course leader for help finding someone external to the movement I serve who had the skills and experience to help me. That decision couldn't have come at a better time as I was navigating a difficult season, and my coach was there to ask me the right questions. Though on occasions they were uncomfortable to answer, they did what they were supposed to and unlocked helpful conversation that gave fresh shape to my journey and the encouragement and support I needed.

We were never built to travel life alone. Right from the beginning God fashioned humankind to live and work together. Eve and Adam were created to help each other. The reference to man in Genesis 2:18 is not talking about one specific gender cleaning up after the other. It was showing us the partnership that is reflected in the Trinity modelled for human beings. The best is brought out of us by the relationships we have.

That is why I urge you to find mentors and coaches. These are people who have walked the long road of Christian leadership ahead of you. They have experienced some of the pitfalls and learned how to determine the weight that they should not be carrying. They can advise you, pray for you and teach you how to judge what parts of the shepherd-leader life we need to persevere in and what we need to lay down on the roadside as we journey forward.

All the best athletes in the world, in whatever sport, have had coaches. Often the athlete surpasses the achievements of their coach as they take heed to their guidance. I thank God for the people who have spoken into my life. For the times when they warned me of the dangers of trying to carry too much, and even times when they spurred me on to pick up weights I didn't imagine were possible for me to carry. We must always remember that we lead for an audience of one. When other stages may place us in front of tens, hundreds or thousands of people, it helps us carry the weight to know that the one who called us may just be much easier to please than those who follow us.

9
WOUNDS AND SCARS

The curry house was busy that evening, steam rising from dishes of tikka masala and naan bread, as I listened to a story that would break any pastor's heart. These weren't just any pastor's parents – they were battle-worn shepherds themselves, carrying wounds still fresh like the steaming rice and curry in front of us. I had come expecting a simple dinner before speaking at their son's church. Instead, I found myself witness to a story that echoes through churches across the world: the story of shepherds who were turned on by their sheep.

Leadership wounds cut deepest in places we least expect them – not in corporate boardrooms or political arenas, but in the very churches meant to offer healing. Behind pulpits and in prayer rooms, well-meaning leaders who genuinely pour out their lives for others often suffer in silence, their stories buried beneath Sunday smiles and worship songs. This couple's tale was painfully familiar – a younger leader they had mentored, in whom they had invested years of guidance and love, had turned their legacy into a weapon against them. Their protégé and supporters had crafted a narrative that transformed these seasoned servants into villains, forcing them to leave the very community they had spent years building.

In an earlier chapter I rightly focused on the fact that many people in church congregations are hurt by those who lead them. But it would be an inaccurate and biased picture of the church if I did not equally talk about the hurt that shepherd-leaders experience from those who they are seeking to lead. In a community that is designed to be seasoned by grace we have too often not demonstrated enough of that great virtue to one another, certainly not in the way that Christ has shown us such 'amazing grace' at our darkest and worst moments.

But it isn't just the pain shepherd-leaders experience at the hands of others in the church. Many are navigating awful situations in their family life. They may be experiencing difficulties in their marriage, or their relationships with their children or wider family are broken. They are battling health issues, or mental health challenges. They are struggling financially, sometimes because of low pay in the ministry and may be burdened by years of debt. They are human. They experience life just like everyone else does. But maybe their greatest challenge is that they are expected to rise above everything that those they lead struggle with, whilst in pain themselves.

HOW WOUNDS HAPPEN

There are several ways that leadership wounds happen. They correlate with the way that physical wounds happen, though the way they are treated back to health is very different.

Intentional attacks

These are wounds inflicted deliberately, often violently. A visit to your local A&E department late on a Saturday night might see victims waiting for treatment to their wounds received in a drunken brawl or, worse, through some mindless mugging. Sadly, we see the effects of a violent society all around us and many people have been deeply wounded by intentional attacks on them. But this happens in relationships and in leadership too. There are occasions when shepherd-leaders are on the receiving end of intentional attacks. They are not physical attacks but many of us have found that emotional wounds take much longer to heal than physical wounds do.

The hardest thing for many shepherd-leaders to deal with is that these kinds of attacks are so intentional. It leaves a sense of bewilderment amid the pain. All leaders make mistakes. All leaders are misunderstood at some point. All leaders fail to communicate as well as they could on occasions.

Even the greatest of spiritual leaders was not immune to the piercing arrows of criticism and character assassination. The apostle Paul's letters reveal a leader intimately acquainted with the sting of slander and the weight of wrongful accusations. His raw honesty pulls back the curtain on the painful reality of leadership in the early church. Some dismissed him as 'the scum of the earth, the garbage of the world', yet he responded with surprising gentleness, choosing to 'answer kindly' in the face of slander (1 Corinthians 4:12-13).

Critics attacked everything from his physical attributes to his speaking abilities, sneering that while 'his letters are weighty and forceful... in person he is unimpressive and his speaking amounts to nothing' (2 Corinthians 10:10). They questioned his credentials, labelled him an inferior apostle, and mocked him as an unskilled speaker (2 Corinthians 11:5-6). The attacks grew so severe that Paul was forced to defend not only his apostleship but the very gospel message he preached (Galatians 1:11-24).

Not all wounds, though, arise from such acts of violence or wilful intent. Much more of the pain in life is seemingly incidental and unintentional. We all experience smaller wounds that sometimes don't even involve other people.

Accidental injuries

I'm sure we've all tripped over something or cut ourselves in food preparation. Many a wound happens quite incidentally with no intention involved at all. Accidents happen often when we least expect them, and they can cause wounds that take time to heal. At times our own insecurities as a leader mean that things said to us take on proportions that were not intended in what was spoken. There may have been a lack of understanding or wisdom. But many people wouldn't have known the difficulties we were facing at the time, and therefore the effects of their words or actions upon us, however unintentional they were.

The truth is our hearts are very tender places. They are the engine room of our thoughts and emotions and when we feel fragile, some simple innocuous things that happened to us can feel wounding. Comments that were made might have seemed humorous to the person speaking but they may well have felt like criticism to the leader receiving them. Maybe not being invited to a big birthday celebration of someone in the church was not deliberate, but it can hurt when you see on social media that all the other leaders and their spouses were invited. The challenge for shepherd-leaders is that not many who they lead will understand how insecure they often feel in the role, and so such accidental injuries are in so many ways inevitable.

The very nature of what leadership is brings about tensions that are going to cause some degree of pain. Many people don't like change, and many others are frustrated by the status quo. So which group are you going to please and which group are you going to disappoint? These are the unavoidable stresses placed on the relationships between a shepherd-leader and those they lead. Samuel Chand describes this tension well in his book, *Leadership Pain*: 'All leadership is a magnet for pain, which comes in many forms. We catch flak for bad decisions because people blame us, and we get criticism even for good decisions because we've changed the beloved status quo.'[34]

Even small accidental injuries are at risk of infection if left untreated. Just because something seems innocuous does not mean that it doesn't need treatment. I have met some leaders who sought to brush aside, or even hide, their smaller wounds without realising they had become infected with greater negativity, disappointment and frustration. This then affected their capacity to lead with grace and humility.

The final way that wounds happen is so very different. It is intentional and very deliberate. But it illustrates that compassion requires much more than a listening ear. It sometimes requires decisive action to get to the real root of why a wound, pain or hurt exists.

Surgical procedure

This kind of wound is fundamentally different from the others we've discussed. Unlike wounds inflicted through conflict or accident, surgical wounds are designed to bring freedom from pain. The surgeon's scalpel may cut deep, but it does so with purpose and precision – to remove cancer, repair broken bones or transplant a failing heart. This deliberate wounding comes from a place of compassion and skill, aimed entirely at healing.

I came to understand this profound difference through my own journey of healing. Several years ago, I was deeply wounded by a family member – not a church member or fellow leader, but someone close to home. While I can't share all the details, I was caught in the aftermath of a situation that caused devastating pain to many. The impact ran deeper than I initially recognised, leaving me with wounds that needed more than just time to heal.

It was during this season of processing my own pain that I found unexpected insight in an unlikely place. One evening, while watching one of the medical documentaries I'm oddly fascinated by (much to my wife Amanda's dismay), I witnessed something that would reshape my understanding of how God heals our deepest wounds.

This documentary told the story of ground-breaking surgery being conducted at the Queen Elizabeth Hospital in Selly Oak, Birmingham. My fascination wasn't only the procedures themselves, but the fact that we live three miles from this hospital, and I've spent many hours walking its corridors to visit church members in the multiple wards that form this huge healthcare facility.

The one scene that I will never forget from this TV programme told the story of a lady who had been crippled by a massive sarcoma tumour for some considerable time and the operation she was facing was in every way a life and death situation. As the clinical team met in the operating theatre moments before the patient was wheeled in for her under-anaesthetic procedure, the lead clinician turned to one of the surgeons and asked a very simple question, *'How long will the procedure take?'* The surgeon's response hit me deep in my soul and spoke to my woundedness. He simply said, *'Until it is finished.'* In that moment two dramatic things happened within me.

Firstly, I was overwhelmed with admiration for the whole clinical team when it transpired that the operation took twelve hours. For a few moments I thought of all the things I had been doing in the previous twelve hours. I couldn't imagine the levels of concentration and compassion that were necessary to successfully remove this huge tumour and give this wonderful lady a fresh opportunity at life. But a far greater thing happened in my soul as I felt clearly the voice of the Holy Spirit say to me, *'The same is true for you, son. I will continue to work in you until you are whole, until it is finished'.* I am not at all embarrassed to say that I sat weeping as the clock ticked past 11.00pm and I felt the presence of God surround me and comfort me.

You see, the cut of the divine physician's scalpel is the most healing experience we could have. Allowing him to access the areas of our hearts that have been damaged in seeking to love and lead people is the most liberating thing we can do.

I have had more occasions when I have chosen to lay my life before the divine physician and allow him to cut away at my disappointment, bitterness and regret. Like all post-surgical patients, I have found that healing takes time, but with every week that passes his peace replaces my pain. What is essential for all shepherd-leaders is an honesty in recognising the need for healing, and the intentional pursuit of this.

HEALING: HOW TO FIND IT?

Hiding the deep issues of one's heart does nothing more than suppress the very opportunity for healing to bring about the kind of sustainable and resilient leadership that is needed for those who daily lay down their lives in ministering to others. I remember hearing the evangelist Reinhard Bonnke say: 'God is not repelled by your weaknesses; he is attracted to them.' I found that so helpful and liberating. It helped me realise that the Lord wants to engage with me in my weakness. Therefore, it's critical we explore some of the ways in which shepherd-leaders can intentionally seek healing for those invisible yet real wounds that can sit very deeply in our souls.

Rest and solitude

At the heart of pastoral healing lies the biblical principle of Sabbath rest. Jesus himself modelled this essential practice, as recorded by the gospel writer Mark, 'Very early in the morning, while it was still dark, Jesus got up, left the house and went off to a solitary place, where he prayed' (Mark 1:35). This isn't merely a suggestion but a divine pattern for spiritual leaders. Regular, intentional solitude provides the space needed for emotional wounds to surface and begin healing. Pastors must recognise that setting aside time for rest isn't self-indulgent but rather an act of stewardship of their calling.

Following Jesus' example of withdrawing with his disciples for rest (Mark 6:31), periodic sabbaticals offer opportunities for deeper restoration. These extended breaks allow time for physical rest, emotional processing, and spiritual renewal beyond what regular weekly rhythms can provide. Whilst taking a sabbatical every seven years is a great thing to do, life happens in the gaps, and learning to find peace and rest in the smaller gaps in life is of huge importance to those who are committed to living the calling on their lives. After all, surely the most important thing we can do with our time is to be with Jesus. I love what John Mark Comer says in his book, *Practising the Way*, 'The reward for following Jesus is, well Jesus. It's the sheer joy of friendship with him.'[35] Is there anyone you could meet whose company would be more healing than Jesus'?

In fact, he knows you better than you know yourself. Maybe you could even pause now from reading. Take just a few moments, if necessary, and ask the Saviour to draw close to you. Ask him to reassure you that he not only knows and understands but is with you *'until it is finished',* until your wounds are healed.

Professional support

While many shepherd-leaders excel at counselling others, they often hesitate to seek counselling themselves. Professional Christian counselling offers a unique combination of clinical expertise and spiritual understanding. This confidential space allows pastors to process their experiences without fear of judgement or congregational impact. A counsellor can help identify patterns of stress, develop coping strategies, and work through deep-seated wounds from ministry experiences. Sadly, I fear there is still a stigma among some leaders about professional counselling. Over recent years I have come to respect deeply the value and benefit of professional counselling.

I referred earlier to my own struggles some years ago, and in late 2019, when those emotional wounds were having a greater impact, I valued the advice of a friend who suggested I should seek some professional counselling. I was cautious as I wanted the freedom to completely unpack what was within me, that I didn't even understand myself. I found a local counsellor who wasn't a Christian but whose understanding and professional skill proved hugely beneficial to me, and whilst much of the time was me unloading thoughts and feelings from deep within the reservoir of my own soul, her support and advice gave me a solid footing to move forward.

While professional counselling provides essential clinical support and expertise, healing often requires a complementary network of authentic relationships. The journey from woundedness to wholeness isn't meant to be walked alone, nor should it be limited to the counsellor's office.

Friendships and mentoring

Ministry can be isolating, but it needn't be solitary. Galatians 6:2 instructs believers to 'carry each other's burdens' and so 'fulfil the law of Christ'. This principle takes on special significance in pastoral circles. Friendships provide a unique form of healing through shared experiences and mutual understanding. These relationships offer safe spaces to discuss challenges that might be inappropriate to share within one's congregation. The wisdom of Proverbs identifies how 'iron sharpens iron, so one person sharpens another' (Proverbs 27:17) and speaks directly to the value of mentorship.

Experienced leaders who have weathered similar storms can offer invaluable perspective and guidance. This relationship requires vulnerability – a quality often challenging for leaders but essential for genuine healing. None of us have arrived where we have in leadership without the vital love and support of experienced men and women around us, and if we think we will never need the wisdom of those who have journeyed where we are yet to walk, we are seriously mistaken.

The psalmist says, 'My friends and companions avoid me because of my wounds; my neighbours stay far away' (Psalm 38:11). The psalmist seems to recognise those times when people don't quite understand why we are acting the way we are. They don't know what to say or how to respond to us because we have stepped back from the kind of relationships that could bring healing to our wounds. Even Jesus needed friends. He led a team of twelve but had three who accompanied him on some special ministry trips, and had friends in Lazarus and his sisters, Mary and Martha, with whom he could enjoy meals and relaxation. We all need friends, and we all need seasoned, experienced friends to guide us.

Embracing the work of the Spirit within

Of course, lamenting is not designed of itself to be the answer but to propel us deep into the arms of the Holy Spirit and his tender nursing of our lives. Embrace of God's presence as the Spirit residing within us begins to move in healing is part of the surrender any patient needs to the superior knowledge and skill of a physician. Psalm 147:3 assures us that 'he heals the broken-hearted and binds up their wounds'. These aren't mere platitudes but powerful truths that can sustain leaders through difficult seasons. Regular meditation on the promises reinforces God's presence in times of struggle.

The completed work of the surgeon is often followed with rehabilitation and regular medication to strengthen the clinical work undertaken. I have found the consistency of daily soaking in God's word, even for a short time, is much like daily medication as it works in the unseen of my soul to realign my heart and mind to the truth that is eternal and unchanging.

The healing work that needs to happen in the souls of wounded shepherd-leaders can take much longer than is desired. We have been told that time is a healer, and in many ways that is true. The suggestions above are not quick fixes, because there really are no quick fixes for leadership pain, only the consistency of loyal friends, skilled support and the enduring faithfulness of God in our lives. But in time our wounds can heal, and healed wounds are often referred to as scars – the marks on our skin of where we were once wounded, or where the surgeon has intervened in our medical crisis. But scars are not something we should shy away from. They measure our journey of healing, and they share a vital message. As Tom Nelson observes: 'As leaders, we must acknowledge and embrace our wounds if we are ever to be able to shepherd effectively. It is only through the experience of our own healing through the power of Christ that we can offer that same hope to those we lead.'[36]

DON'T BE ASHAMED OF YOUR SCARS

Have you ever considered how Jesus was healed from the wounds of the cross, but he still had the scars that showed what he had suffered? When he visited doubting Thomas, he invited him to examine his scars.

> *Jesus came and stood among them and said, 'Peace be with you!' Then he said to Thomas, 'Put your finger here; see my hands. Reach out your hand and put it into my side. Stop doubting and believe.* (John 20:26-27)

Those scars were the sign that he had overcome the wounds inflicted on him by the Jewish and Roman authorities. Your scars symbolise what you have overcome. How you have been healed. They say, *'This is how badly I was hurt, but look at what God has done.'* Scars are your testimony of God's ability to heal our wounds. They are part of our life journey and are proof that we are loved by a God who heals internal wounds in a way that no one else can. I carry scars that used to be a wound. I don't feel the same pain anymore, though at times it feels very sore. But I know that God is still working in my heart and mind to bring healing and freedom to me. And I know that he can do the same for you.

I have found that showing my scars to some of those who I am privileged to minister to has been so helpful in encouraging them, that they too can find healing from things that have hurt them so deeply. Many of us are walking testimonies to God's goodness and faithfulness. But I also know that many are suffering silently, feeling that no-one sees or understands the pain they feel within. I hope that in these words you have read you will see hope and find encouragement to speak up to someone you can trust, sharing honestly your need of healing. I pray that you have not let the hurt of what you have experienced become the defining factor in your life journey at this moment. Don't stop believing in a kind, heavenly Father who longs to minister healing into the deepest parts of your soul.

The journey of pastoral healing is neither quick nor simple, but it is essential for sustainable ministry. As I think back to that curry-house conversation, I'm struck by how that couple's story represents both the deep wounds that shepherd-leaders carry and the possibility of healing that lies ahead. Their willingness to share their pain that evening wasn't just an unburdening – it was the beginning of their healing journey.

Over steaming dishes that had grown cold as they spoke, I watched something shift in their expressions. Perhaps it was the simple act of being heard, of having their story acknowledged, that began to lift the weight they carried. They weren't just speaking to me – they were opening their wounds to the Great Physician himself, allowing his healing presence into spaces that had been locked away in silence.

To my fellow shepherd-leaders reading these words: your wounds are seen, your pain is valid, and your healing matters. Don't let the hurt you've experienced become the final chapter of your story. The same God who met us in that curry house, who shows up in hospital corridors and counselling offices, in quiet moments of lament and in conversations with trusted friends – he's waiting to meet you too. Your wounds may be deep, but his healing is deeper still.

Remember, taking care of your own emotional and spiritual health isn't just about survival – it's about stewarding the calling God has placed on your life. And sometimes, that stewardship begins with simply being honest enough to say, like that couple did over the spicy curry dishes, 'We're hurting, but we know the Lord is healing us.'

10
THE SHEPHERD'S SUPERPOWER

Growing up, I wasn't as aware of Marvel or DC Comics superheroes as kids are today. But I did have a hero with the ultimate superpower: Captain Scarlett was indestructible. As Spectrum's most potent agent in their battle against the Mysterons, he repeatedly placed himself in the firing line, secure in the knowledge that their attacks could not prove fatal. He would always return to win the day.

Superheroes with superpowers are more popular than ever in today's media-driven world. From cinema to streaming platforms, there's a huge market for these incredibly expensive productions. Whether it's Spider-Man, Batman, Wonder Woman, Incredible Hulk or Black Panther, these characters dwell in a fantasy world of strength and invincibility that us mere mortals know is far from the realities of our very normal world.

It seems that many who feel trapped in that normality, might dream of the adulation and exploits of the comic-book hero, or even strangely look to a Christian leader to fill the need for inspiration. Some may even read their Bible with this mindset. There are seemingly heroic figures throughout the scriptures. But when we look more into their stories, we see their weaknesses and flaws. Samson, for all his remarkable strength, had a problem with resisting temptation. Gideon didn't even believe that God could use him. Peter's towering confession of Jesus as the Christ at Caesarea Philippi, turns into a blundering denial that he didn't even know Jesus. We are all very human after all. There are no superheroes in real life, just normal people who can sometimes do exceptional things. Likewise, there are no superheroes in the body of Christ, just redeemed people who God uses in very extraordinary ways.

WHAT'S YOUR SUPERPOWER?

I wonder, if I could offer you any superpower as a leader that you wished for, what ability, quality or gift would you choose? To inspire people with brilliance as a preacher, to have incredible insight as a leader, to sing with the voice of an angel or possess the foresight to anticipate the problems you'd want to avoid? Or did you decide that you would choose humility? Is your desire to mirror the same quality that Jesus epitomised as he hung on a Roman cross, vilified and insulted by the baying crowd?

I learned one of the most important lessons of my life as a leader within the first few years of becoming pastor at Christian Life Centre in Birmingham. I was a young, committed leader who wanted to move the church forward. We had seen quite a few people come to faith in Christ and I believed it was important to ensure their early steps in discipleship were secure. I asked one of the young adults in our church, who had recently completed a training school with YWAM, to help me launch a nurture group for these new believers. She enthusiastically accepted the opportunity to support me in doing this, but I had failed to talk with the leader of the small group she was part of, who was also an elder. He was a strong character who I had struggled to relate to, as I felt he would sometimes quite deliberately seek to intimidate me.

As I mingled with people after our evening service, he approached me and launched into a humiliating tirade for not consulting him about my decision to ask Samantha to help me lead this new group. I was caught like the proverbial rabbit in the headlights by his attack on me and uncharacteristically had no ability to meaningfully reply to him. He then left the building, and I stood aware that all eyes were on me. I couldn't get home quick enough as I tried to process the feelings of embarrassment and humiliation.

The next day I spoke with my regional leader who encouraged me to take the opportunity to speak personally to the man who had challenged me so vociferously. The next day I telephoned him to arrange to meet, and plans were made for me to visit his home on the day after that. I could think of little else but this meeting that was going to take place and mentally rehearsed how I would put him in his place and let him know, in no uncertain terms, that his behaviour towards me was unacceptable and disrespectful.

Throughout the morning ahead of the meeting I continued to rehearse my speech, imagining myself sitting in his lounge and confronting him. It was only a five-minute drive from my church office to his home, but my mental preparations for this confrontation continued as I drove the short journey. I remember parking just outside his house and hearing this quiet whisper in my soul simply instruct me, 'Stuart, say sorry.' I knew it was the voice of the Lord because it was so contrary to my own feelings and thoughts. It felt like I was now in disagreeable conversation with the Lord himself, seeking to explain all the reasons why I should confront the man and not cave in to the way he had treated me. The inner voice became stronger and more compelling, and I knew instinctively that to reject it was not the righteous or obedient thing to do.

I rang the doorbell, and the door was opened to me. After the awkward greetings I was guided to the man's lounge. He offered me a drink and then went to the kitchen to make it while I sat on the sofa trying to figure out how I could change the narrative that had been in my head for a few days, to respond immediately to the prompting of the Spirit within. When he returned, I simply told him I wanted to unreservedly apologise for not considering the need to talk to him before inviting somebody from his group to help me launch the new group. I will never forget the moment as all that tension and even aggression in my soul disappeared, and his surprise meant that he seemed speechless himself when he, too, may well have been rehearsing his arguments for challenging me.

I learned that day that a humble apology is more powerful than a well-articulated argument. He hadn't conducted himself well that previous

Sunday evening, but neither had I for nearly seventy-two hours since. I'd contemplated behaviour that was not befitting of my responsibilities as a leader. Attitudes and actions that did not sit comfortably with the call on my life to model the humility of Jesus. All it took was an apology and we were able to find a way beyond our disagreement and hurt. That lesson has guided many moments in my ministry and leadership since. Saying sorry has never seemed defeat to me; sometimes it's the most appropriate response for me as a leader to make. It's not humiliating to acknowledge you were wrong – it is honest.

JESUS THE SUPERHERO

If the Bible does have a superhero, then it only has one: Jesus. There may be some who don't like my use of this idiom to describe Jesus, and I completely understand. What I mean is that the enormity of what Jesus did in his mission to earth cannot be truly understood in the context of life on this planet. His purpose in coming to our earth was of eternal and cosmic significance, and his battle with the powers of darkness are in so many ways the very plot line that the human soul seems to know instinctively. The theme of good versus evil sits at the heart of all those comic hero films and many a science fiction or fantasy film too. For every superhero there is usually an arch enemy. An opponent who wants to wreak havoc but who usually ends up losing, much to the delight of the superhero's adoring public.

The beautiful irony of this analogy is that the superpower Jesus carried is the antithesis of what the Jewish people expected in their Messiah. When they were looking for a warrior to destroy their Roman enemies, Jesus came as the suffering servant that the prophets foretold. He declared that he had 'not come to be served, but to serve, and to give his life as a ransom for many' (Matthew 20:28). He surrendered to the Jewish guards in Gethsemane and stayed silent when falsely accused of blasphemy by the religious authorities, and Peter took out his sword to attack those coming to arrest Jesus, presumably because he couldn't understand why Jesus was allowing this unjust arrest to take place.

When Jesus picked up the ear of the guard assaulted by Peter and returned it to its original location on the side of the guard's head, he was revealing that human violence was not the reaction he wanted to his willing surrender to the Jewish guards. He did not come to earth to win a victory with swords or clubs. His pathway to victory was surrender and humility.

When Paul wrote to the Philippians, he summarised this most astonishing characteristic of Jesus in what some Bible commentators think may have been an ancient hymn.

> *In your relationships with one another, have the same mindset as Christ Jesus: who, being in very nature God, did not consider equality with God something to be used to his own advantage; rather, he made himself nothing by taking the very nature of a servant, being made in human likeness. And being found in appearance as a man, he humbled himself by becoming obedient to death – even death on a cross!* (Philippians 2:5-8)

Those words, 'He humbled himself', have so impacted me in recent years that I did something my kids could not believe was possible. After having had an opinion about tattoos that was certainly not positive for most of my life, I had three H's tattooed on my inner right wrist. For a few months before my apparent midlife crisis, I had been challenged with the intentionality of Jesus' humility. I knew that this wasn't matched in my life often enough, and I was challenged about how easy it is as a leader to become entitled, and how much I really didn't want to be that way. My tattoo serves as a daily reminder of what the Saviour did for me, but also how he did it.

'He humbled himself' is one of the greatest statements about Jesus in all of scripture, and something shepherd-leaders need to model. It isn't easy being intentional about humility because it can seem false to some people when a leader tries to live in this kind of way. It's a little like the humorous adage, 'I'm humble and proud of it', which is in every way an oxymoron. In today's church there is a real cry for authenticity. A younger generation have grown up in the church who are inspired more by authenticity than invincibility. It's not as impressive as some leaders think to appear to be impenetrable by the negative circumstances of life and leadership. One of my friends, Simon Foster, once said to me that 'people want their leaders vulnerable, they just don't want them weak', and I understand what he meant.

Too many leaders want to be strong, and almost invincible. They wouldn't use the word power because we have realised there are so many painful consequences when it is misused. That is why we must challenge the superhero notion in Christian leadership and celebrate virtues that have been buried beneath the pursuit of significance. Is strength really the superpower of godly shepherd-leaders, or is it humility? Do we have some things to learn about humility that have been ignored for too long?

There have been moments in pastoral life that really humbled me. Some have been in the mistakes I have made; others have been as I have walked with people through their pain and suffering as their pastor. One of those times was when Andy met with a tragic experience that has shaped his life, and that of his wife Emma and their family, and left him with clinically diagnosed Locked-in syndrome.

I will always remember 1st November 2011. I remember where I was when my assistant Pastor Carla called me to tell me Andy had had a stroke, and the events of that day as they unfolded into the evening when the final catastrophic stroke left us praying for Andy's life to continue. In the book

Andy wrote to record this event and its consequences, he recalls a moment between him and me as he lay unable to move or communicate: 'During another of these clear moments I remember Pastor Stuart asking me if I wanted to fight on and to blink once if I did. I gave a single strong blink.'[37] That blink inspired me to call the church to prayer. I had never known such a commitment and passion to pray for someone as our church experienced over those weeks and months when there was huge uncertainty about Andy's health and future.

Eventually, Andy left the Queen Elizabeth Hospital, Birmingham, and went into Moseley Hall Hospital for rehabilitation, which itself was a disastrous experience for Andy as the staff and the hospital were inadequately equipped to help or support him. After ten months Andy finally got home on 2nd September 2012. He immediately threw a party and invited many of us as friends and family to be together and celebrate his homecoming. It's hard to party when you can see someone you care about struggle with paralysis from the neck down and wholly dependent on carers, family and friends. But Andy continued to inspire me and so many other people with his courage and faith amidst what were huge questions, and at times huge doubts.

My visits to Andy would often be discussions with him when he was trying to understand where God was in his crisis. I never saw these times as frustrating but a critically important part of loving and supporting Andy and Emma through something of which I could not begin to imagine the difficulty. We are not supposed to have all the answers for people's tragedy. I learned through my discussions with Andy how Christian platitudes can be so distressing for people trapped in situations they cannot extricate themselves from. Sometimes engaging with their doubts and trying to shine just the smallest light of hope is the best that we can offer.

My friends Andy and Emma have continued to defy the odds set against them. Andy studied for six years to attain a theology degree, which is a stunning achievement. He and Emma set up a business providing holiday accommodation specifically designed for people with disabilities. Andy did a further university validated course in counselling, and they help to lead a small group in the church they are now committed to. Maybe the greatest joy and miracle, though, is that Andy and Emma have been blessed with two amazing children, Samuel and Charlie. Today they navigate the challenges of parenthood together with no significant change to Andy's physical condition.

There were many times I didn't know what to say or how to help. But I do believe that God graced us with his presence every time we met to talk through a challenging situation Andy was facing or just simply for us to share a meal together. This was what I found so humbling. That God places us in people's lives not always for the joyous moments, but to support them in the tragedies they face.

Walking alongside Andy and Emma through their journey taught me profound lessons about authentic humility in leadership. Their story illustrates that true pastoral care often means simply being present, acknowledging our limitations, and letting go of the need to have all the answers. These experiences have helped me recognise that genuine humility isn't just a noble ideal – it has specific, identifiable characteristics that we can observe and cultivate. Just as precious metals carry distinctive marks that verify their authenticity, there are certain hallmarks that indicate true humility in a shepherd-leader's life.

FOUR HALLMARKS OF HUMILITY

Just as a jeweller knows precisely what marks authenticate precious metals, we need clear indicators that distinguish genuine humility from its counterfeits. True humility in leadership isn't about appearing weak or diminishing our calling. Rather, it's about exhibiting authentic Christlike character that others can recognise and trust. These four hallmarks aren't exhaustive, but they represent essential qualities that set apart leaders who have embraced Jesus' model of humble shepherding. They serve as touchstones against which we can examine our own hearts and leadership patterns.

An identity rooted in Christ

Humility means you have a calm and accepting idea of who you are. Humility is not a self-loathing; humility is knowing that we are accepted by God for who we are and that he is working in us to make us more like Christ. The world is a better place if leaders are not striving to be something that they are not. When they're not trampling over others to achieve their ends and desires. But they are men and women who have learned in their calling that they are children of God, and their identity is secured in Christ's validation of them and not the affirmation that they might seek in the approval of others.

A genuine self-awareness

Humility means being conscious of your strengths and your weaknesses. Humble shepherds don't try to project an exaggerated view of themselves. They're not always seeking to tell inflated stories of their significance or achievements, rather they recognise that any fruitfulness they have seen in life and ministry is because of God's goodness, grace and patience with each of us. Truly humble shepherd-leaders are aware of their own frailties and are willing to take responsibility for the mistakes that they make. The apostle Paul seems to have lived within an acute awareness that as much as God worked in and through his life, there were inherent challenges in his humanness that he battled with regularly. 'He said to me, "My grace is sufficient for you, for my power is made perfect in weakness." Therefore I will boast all the more gladly about my weaknesses so that Christ's power may rest on me' (2 Corinthians 12:9).

A genuine self-awareness creates an opportunity to see God more deeply at work in our character and in the outworking of our ministry and leadership. Those shepherd-leaders who understand the power of humility do not hide their personal vulnerabilities but allow God to work through them by his grace, so that others can find deep connection in relationship with them as a leader, and then themselves similarly seek the power of Christ to work within them, bringing about the kind of change that only he can.

A beautiful selflessness

Humility is about seeing that everyone have the same intrinsic value and importance as each other. It is recognising that we need to dismantle hierarchical notions that elevate leaders to positions of importance that are not recognised in the models given to us in scripture. Too often Christian leaders have sought the prominence and profile that is seen in our secular society, without recognising that these models of leadership often succeed only because others are considered of a lesser value or importance than those who might have achieved some degree of high office. As Brad Lomenick has said, 'Humble leaders are willing to pass on the credit but absorb the criticism, push others higher while making themselves lower, and put the team's desires ahead of their own. A leader's job is to shepherd, not necessarily to always shine.'[38]

There are such inequalities in our society, but the heart of the Christian message is still that all men and women have the same value before God, and therefore before each other. In fact, the countercultural message of Jesus teaches us to place greater value on others than we do even on ourselves. Paul also reflects this in his letters. 'Do nothing out of selfish ambition or vain conceit. Rather, in humility value others above yourselves' (Philippians 2:3).

A sincere gratitude

Humility recognises that we own nothing, and all that we have is a gift from God. One of the enemies of humility is entitlement; the feeling that I have the right to do as I wish or benefit in some way more generously than others. Such illusions create destructive patterns in the thinking of many a leader, who see others with greater benefits or more significant opportunities than they have and fail to recognise the goodness of God in their own life and circumstances.

I have learned how important it is to create moments when I simply sit and thank God for his kindness and generosity in my life. I think about my wife and her enduring loyalty and love for me over the years we have shared the gift of marriage that God gave to us. I think of my children who fill my heart with so much joy, and my grandchildren for whom I cannot even find the words to describe the depth of my love. I think of my friends and colleagues in ministry. I think of the blessings of health, that even though my body is ageing I have the strength to enjoy the wonderful world God has placed me in and the opportunities he has given to me. I think you get the message. There is more to give thanks to God for than we can ever imagine. Thankfulness is the life we have been called to. Once more Paul seeks to stir great virtues in us when he tells us, 'Give thanks in all circumstances; for this is God's will for you in Christ Jesus' (1 Thessalonians 5:18).

The way of humility is ultimately the way of the cross. Shepherd-leaders are not superheroes and were never called to be. We are not impervious to attack and cannot just deflect any bullets as if they mean nothing. We do not live in a DC Comics or Marvel world. We live in a real world where people hurt, and people struggle. They need leaders who are not trying to hide their vulnerabilities and challenges, but they are shepherds who honestly face up to the struggles involved in loving and leading people, and seek daily the grace and strength that can only be accessed through the Spirit of God dwelling in each of us. They are humble because they know they need Jesus daily, and this alone is enough to inspire others to follow.

11
TTHE UNWRITTEN CHAPTER

When Charles Dickens died in 1870, he left his final novel, *The Mystery of Edwin Drood*, unfinished. The manuscript ends mid-story, with countless possibilities for how the tale might have concluded. Like Dickens' unfinished work, our lives and leadership journeys are stories still being written. Each day, we author new pages through our actions, decisions and interactions with others. While we may not be putting pen to paper, we are crafting our legacy in how we lead, serve and impact those around us.

There's an old English idiom used to describe someone whose actions are predictable: 'I can read him like a book.' In many ways, our lives as leaders are indeed like books – open for others to read through our consistent patterns of behaviour and decision-making. Yet unlike a printed novel, our story isn't fixed. We have the remarkable opportunity to shape the chapters ahead.

As shepherd-leaders, we face a crucial question: what will the remaining chapters of our leadership story contain? The pages ahead are blank, waiting to be filled with either intentional growth and positive impact, or stagnation and missed opportunities. The choice of how this story unfolds lies largely in our hands.

There are still chapters of our lives that are yet to be written. Depending on your age, that might be many, but for some of us it will be fewer. Let's be honest, we are each writing our autobiography, every day we live. We may not be picking up paper and pen or sitting with a keyboard and mouse, but our every action is recording the story of our lives. They are the things that people will remember about us or may even share in a eulogy or tribute at our funeral. As we consider the story we're leaving behind, it's worth asking: what story are we actively writing today?

YOUR AUTOBIOGRAPHY IS BEING WRITTEN

Life is the great unfinished novel. I'm not sure anyone completes every chapter of their lives in the way they had planned, and some have no sense of what they want their life to be and live in that somewhat fatalistic *que sera, sera* – whatever will be, will be.

I've learned a few important lessons in the last few years of my life. They have been taught in the classroom of both blessing and disappointment. My tutors have been my experiences and my reflections upon them. These lessons are not particularly profound, but they have been life changing for me. Two key lessons I've learned very clearly in the most recent season of my life are:

I can choose the person that I want to be, and I can choose the kind of leader I want to be.

These are the unwritten chapters of my life. But they are also the unwritten chapters of your life. I've met many people, some of them being leaders, who seem to believe that there is nothing they can do about the life they are living. I don't believe that. I wish I had learned these lessons much earlier in my life and ministry. They would have saved me from quite a few mistakes along the way. Essentially, I have learned that with the help of God the Spirit living in me, I can have far greater choice over my actions and reactions than I had previously felt was possible. For example:

I can choose how I respond to disappointment

I can choose how I respond to criticism

I can choose how I respond to opposition

I can choose how I respond to failure

I can choose how I respond to mistakes

I can choose how I respond to relational breakdown

I can choose how I respond to success

David's journey as a shepherd-leader exemplifies these choices in action. When faced with Saul's jealousy and persecution, he chose mercy over vengeance (1 Samuel 24:1-7). When confronted with his own failure by Nathan the prophet, he chose humility and repentance over denial (2 Samuel 12:1-13). Even in his finest moments as king, he chose to attribute success to God rather than claim personal glory (2 Samuel 5:12). Each choice shaped not only his leadership but the entire nation he shepherded.

The choices we make represent more than just personal willpower or determination. The God who lives within us is working constantly to shape us more into the image of his Son, Jesus. Jesus chose how to respond to the great human injustice of the cross, 'Father, forgive them, for they do not know what they are doing' (Luke 23:34).

While Jesus modelled this transformative power of choice for us, many leaders today take a different path. Some shepherd-leaders choose to ignore the opportunity for reflection and learning. They refuse to address their attitudes and to change their ways of behaving. Then they want to blame everybody else when things go wrong, or when they fail. The chapters yet to be written in our lives are for us to author with the help of the Spirit. This doesn't mean we are the god of our lives, it's recognising that we already have a framework for what our attitudes and actions should look like: it's Jesus. The truth is that we can choose how much like him we want to be.

Throughout this book I have sought to explain what I believe shepherd-leadership looks like and why I believe it's so important. My aim has been to inspire you as experienced or prospective leaders, to see the power there is in deep connection with those who we lead. I've also attempted to identify several of the challenging aspects of the life of a shepherd-leader, because I know it's not a simple or convenient life for those who respond to God's call.

There is huge encouragement for leaders to develop greater emotional intelligence or self-awareness. However, I think the problem isn't becoming more aware of how I think, feel or behave as a leader; it's knowing what to do with that awareness. It's so much easier to push any revelation we discover about ourselves to the back of our minds, and to choose not to be intentional about change in our lives. That is where we can fail. Shepherd-leadership will expose us to ourselves regularly. What will you do with what you discover? This self-discovery, however challenging, opens the door to something powerful: the opportunity for growth at any stage of our journey.

IT'S NEVER TOO LATE TO GROW

As I write, I am conscious that there may be some who have reflected on past mistakes or even current attitudes they know they are carrying, which hinder them from being the kind of shepherd-leader that we know church communities need. That's why I wanted to write this chapter and call it 'The Unfinished Chapter', because I wanted to create an awareness that though you cannot change your yesterday, you can change your tomorrow. There are still chapters in your life to be written. You can be intentional about the growth and development of your discipleship with Jesus and your leadership among his people.

I'm reminded on occasions of Paul's statement: 'I can do all this through him who gives me strength' (Philippians 4:13). Whilst Paul is talking about how he had learned to be content in whatever circumstances he found himself in, his words also remind us that we do not walk this life alone. The promise of Jesus to always be with us is fulfilled by the residing presence of the Holy Spirit within us. This removes our opportunity to excuse ourselves from the possibility of writing a new chapter in our life or leadership.

You may have made mistakes. You may even have done so knowingly. Yet this wonderful truth remains: God is good, and he is gracious. You can pick up the pen again and begin to write a new chapter in your life. Some of the best leaders I know have determined that they are not going to stop growing. They make choices to listen and to learn. They realise that they are not the finished novel, and that real growth is in the stretch; the way we extend ourselves into developing and maturing.

When I turned fifty years old, I realised that I needed something else to stretch me. I had learned and grown as a leader over the decades and was stepping into significant responsibility within Elim that would stretch my leadership capacity. But there was a hunger for something more, and so I enrolled on a Masters course at Regents Theological College. I hadn't done formal studies for thirty years, and to be honest the Bible college diploma I'd studied was not anywhere near as robust as a formal theological degree.

The studies were a stretch for me. There were late nights – after a long day's work – to complete assignments and many times I thought I could not complete the academic requirements of the course. But I did, and three years later graduated along with a great group of people who I got to know during the process. It's never too late to learn and it's never too late to grow.

The apostle Paul, despite his extensive training and experience, maintained a learner's heart throughout his ministry. Writing to the Philippians from prison he expressed that he had not yet arrived at his goal but was pressing on towards what lay ahead (Philippians 3:12-14). Even after establishing numerous churches and writing much of the New Testament, he requested books and parchments to continue his study (2 Timothy 4:13). Like Paul, shepherd-leaders recognise that there is always more to learn, always room to grow deeper in understanding and effectiveness.

WHAT WILL YOUR LEGACY BE?

My prayer is that you will be inspired to love and lead people from a place of security, humility and generosity. It really is the most profound thing we could ever experience to partner with the Good Shepherd in finding lost sheep and rearing them to be healthy and reproductive so that the flock of God grows and grows.

Your legacy will not be the buildings you have built, the messages you have preach or the books you have written. It will be the people you have loved and the way you have led them. Consider how Jesus invested in his disciples. He didn't leave behind buildings or written treatises; instead, his legacy lived on through the transformed lives of those he shepherded. When reinstating Peter after his denial, Jesus didn't ask about his administrative abilities or theological knowledge, but rather, 'Do you love me?' followed by the command to 'Feed my sheep' (John 21:15-17). This pattern shows us that shepherd-leadership is fundamentally about loving God and caring for his people.

Your legacy will not be measured in sermons preached or buildings raised, but in lives transformed through your shepherd's heart. Every person you've mentored, every team member you've developed, every soul you've comforted in a crisis – these are the living chapters of your leadership story. They are walking testimonies to the power of shepherd-leadership.

Today, you stand at a crossroads. Before you is an empty page, waiting for your next chapter. Will you write it with intentionality and purpose? Will you pursue growth with the same passion you wish to see in those you lead? The shepherd's staff is in your hands – it can be a symbol of stagnation, of merely maintaining what exists, or it can become a tool of transformation, guiding both you and your flock towards greater heights.

Remember, the Good Shepherd didn't just maintain his flock – he laid down his life to see it flourish. Your calling is no less profound. Every choice you make, every skill you develop, every relationship you nurture adds another line to your leadership story. Make it one worth reading. Make it one worth following.

The pen is in your hand. The page is before you. Your next chapter begins now.

What will you write?

ENDNOTES

1. https://churchanswers.com/blog/the-new-mid-size-church-advantages/#:~:text=It's%20 also%20worth%20noting%20that,250%20people%20would%20feel%20large (accessed 2nd October 2024).

2. Brad Lomenick, *H3 Leadership: Be Humble. Stay Hungry. Always Hustle* (Nashville, TN: Thomas Nelson, 2015), p.52-53.

3. Jack Hayford, *Pastors of Promise: Pointing to Character and Hope as the Keys to Fruitful Shepherding* (Ventura CA: Regal Books, 1997), p.20.

4. Tom Nelson, *The Flourishing Pastor: Recovering the Lost Art of Shepherd Leadership* (Downers Grove, IL: Inter-Varsity Press, 2021), p.17.

5. Tom Nelson, *The Flourishing Pastor*, p.38.

6. Jack Hayford, *Pastors of Promise*, p.21.

7. Jamie Swalm, *Shepherd Leadership in the Scriptures: A Biblical Study of Shepherd Leadership in the Old and New Testaments* (2019), p.6.

8. Phillip Keller, *The Shepherd Trilogy* (Grand Rapids, MI: Zondervan, 1996), p.74.

9. Jack Hayford, *Pastors of Promise*, p.24.

10. Phillip Keller, *The Shepherd Trilogy*, p.10.

11. Frank Damazio, *The Making of a Leader: Biblical Leadership Principles for Today's Leaders* (City Bible Publishing, 1988), p.102.

12. Blaine McCormick and David Davenport, *Shepherd Leadership: Wisdom for Leaders from Psalm 23* (San Francisco, CA: Jossey-Bass, 2003), p.2.

13. Phil Pringle, *You the Leader* (Australia: Whitaker House Publishing, 2005), p.126.

14. Phillip Keller, *The Shepherd Trilogy*, p.54-55.

15. John Maxwell, *The 21 Indispensable Qualities of a Leader: Becoming the Person Others Will Want to Follow* (Nashville, TN: Thomas Nelson, 1999), p.4.

16. Warren Wiersbe, *The Strategy of Satan: How to Detect and Defeat Him* (Wheaton, IL: Tyndale House Publishers, 1979), p.89.

17. Eugene H. Peterson, *The Contemplative Pastor* (Wm. B. Eerdmans Publishing Co.,1989), p.112.

18. Diane Langberg, *Redeeming Power: Understanding Authority and Abuse in the Church* (Grand Rapids, MI: Brazos Press, 2020), p.73.

19. Tom Nelson, *The Flourishing Pastor*, p.101.

20 Peter Scazzero, *The Emotionally Healthy Leader* (Grand Rapids, MI: Zondervan, 2015), p.25.

21 https://theunstuckgroup.com/culture-of-honor/ (accessed 6th July 2024).

22 Tim Keller, *Center Church: Doing Balanced, Gospel-Centered Ministry in Your City* (Grand Rapids, MI: Zondervan, 2012), p.32.

23 https://voices.lifeway.com/church-ministry-leadership/entitlement-is-poisoning-the-church/ (accessed 1st August 2024).

24 Philip Greenslade, *Leadership – Patterns for Biblical Leadership Today* (Uckfield, East Sussex: Marshalls, 1984), p.104.

25 William Barclay, *The Daily Study Bible John Volume 2* (Wells, Somerset: The Saint Andrew Press, 1975), p.139.

26 Rick Warren, *The Purpose Driven Life: What on Earth Am I Here For?* (Grand Rapids, MI: Zondervan, 2002), p.254.

27 https://equip.sbts.edu/article/pastoral-ministry-weightiest-callings/ (accessed 8th August 2024).

28 https://equip.sbts.edu/article/pastoral-ministry-weightiest-callings/ (accessed 8th August 2024).

29 https://careynieuwhof.com/9-hidden-things-that-make-or-break-leaders/ (accessed 8th August 2024).

30 High Halverstadt, *Managing Church Conflict* (Louisville, KY: Westminster/John Knox Press, 1991), p.1.

31 https://equip.sbts.edu/article/pastoral-ministry-weightiest-callings/ (accessed 9th August 2024).

32 Franklin Graham, *Billy Graham in Quotes* (Nashville, TN: Thomas Nelson, 2011), p.126.

33 Brad Lomenick, *H3 Leadership*, p.17-18.

34 Samuel R. Chand, *Leadership Pain: The Classroom for Growth* (Nashville, TN: Thomas Nelson, 2015), p.6.

35 John Mark Comer, *Practising the Way: Be with Jesus. Become Like Him. Do as He Did* (London: SPCK, 2024), p.54.

36 Tom Nelson, *The Flourishing Pastor*, p.104.

37 Andrew Davies, *Pressed But Not Crushed* (Malcolm Down Publishing, 2015), Kindle edition p.35.

38 Brad Lomenick, *H3 Leadership*, p.27.